THE LIBRARY OF CHILDREN'S SONG CLASSICS

COMPILED BY AMY APPLEBY AND PETER PICKOW
EDITED BY LIZ SEELHOFF BYRUM

AMSCO PUBLICATIONS
NEW YORK • LONDON • SYDNEY

to Travis Appleby and his musical dad

Cover illustration by Ellen Appleby
Interior design and layout by Peter Pickow

Order Number AM 90167
US International Standard Book Number: 0.8256.1358.2
UK International Standard Book Number: 0.7119.3235.2

Exclusive Distributors:
Music Sales Corporation
257 Park Avenue South, New York, NY 10010, USA
Music Sales Limited
14-15 Berners Street, London W1T 3LJ, UK
Music Sales Pty Limited
20 Resolution Drive, Caringbah, NSW 2229, Australia

Printed in the EU

FOREWORD

Here is a wonderful collection of songs for children and their families to explore together. *The Library of Children's Song Classics* contains over two hundred all-time favorites in one gigantic volume—an essential addition to any home or school library. Easy-to-read lyrics, piano arrangements, and guitar chords allow everyone to join in the fun. Whether singing, dancing, playing, or resting—children will enjoy hours of musical pleasure in school and at home with this delightfully illustrated volume. Young people of all ages love rhymes and rhythms—especially when they are silly and surprising. Many of the songs which have been selected for this collection will inspire games, dancing, and creative dramatics—from pattycake and peek-a-boo for the very young to skipping rope and circle games for older children. Counting and alphabet songs are also a terrific learning tool for young readers. Think back to your own school days, and you will probably recall singing the ABC's to the tune of "Twinkle, Twinkle, Little Star"—just like your parents and grandparents before you. This volume will evoke a wealth of memories from your own past—and inspire many more in your family's future. You and your kids will recognize many of these wonderful songs as performed by today's popular artists on recordings, as well as radio and television programs for children. We've also included many song surprises which will be a real pleasure to discover together.

When we sing together at school, a special bond is formed—and any tears and fears are soon forgotten. Mothers and fathers have always known about the magical power of song to soothe the fussy baby—or calm the fears of a child when there are monsters in the closet. A simple song is also a great way to enhance science and reading skills—whether learning the names of animals and plants, the instruments of the orchestra—or understanding the calendar year. Songs of home and country also have the precious power to strengthen a child's sense of family and patriotism. Songs from other lands help introduce children to ideas, holidays, and customs different from their own.

The names of many of the composers and lyricists whose work is included in this song treasury are unknown. In fact, many of these songs were clearly made up by children and passed along in backyards and playgrounds throughout the world. While the origins of some songs are known, others are adaptations of traditional or classical tunes, themes, and poetry. Although this is a fascinating field of study for some, for the purposes of this volume, historical information has been omitted.

Every parent and teacher knows the importance of music in a child's life. Children express themselves through word and song as a natural extension of early language development. Singing is terrific fun, but it is also perhaps one of the most powerful skills that a child can possess. Teach a child a song, and you will provide him or her with a pathway to self-confidence, creativity, and joy. Spend a moment to make music with your family, and you will enjoy an experience that will always be remembered.

Liz Seelhoff Byrum, M.A.
Early Childhood Education Specialist
New York City

TABLE OF CONTENTS

ANIMAL SONGS

The Animal Song

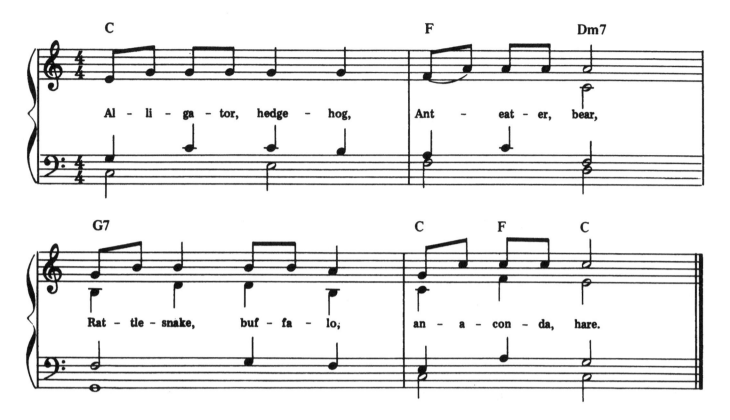

Al - li - ga - tor, hedge - hog, Ant - eat - er, bear,

Rat - tle - snake, buf - fa - lo; an - a - con - da, hare.

Extra Verses

Bullfrog, woodchuck, wolverine, goose,
Whipporwill, chipmunk, jackal, moose.

Mud turtle, whale, glowworm, bat,
Salamander, snail, Maltese cat.

Black squirrel, coon, opossum, wren,
Red squirrel, loon, South Guinea hen.

Reindeer, blacksnake, ibex, nightingale,
Martin, wild drake, crocodile, and quail.

House rat, tosrat, white bear, doe,
Chickadee, peacock, bobolink, and crow.

Eagle, kingeron, sheep, duck, and widgeon,
Conger, armadillo, beaver, seal, pigeon.

Mister Rabbit

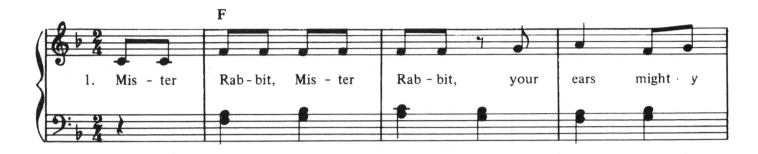

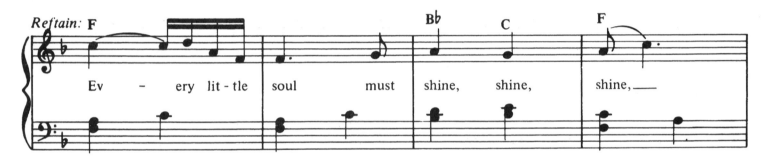

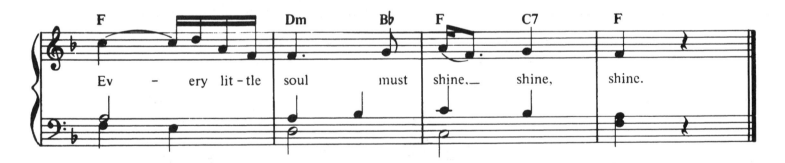

2. Mister Rabbit, Mister Rabbit, your coat mighty gray.
Yes, my Lawd, 'twas made that way.

   REFRAIN:
   Every little soul must shine, shine, shine,
   Every little soul must shine, shine, shine.

4. Mister Rabbit, Mister Rabbit, your tail mighty white.
Yes, my Lawd, and I'm a-getting out of sight.
Refrain:

3. Mister Rabbit, Mister Rabbit, your feet mighty red,
Yes, my Lawd, I'm almost dead.
Refrain:

5. Mister Rabbit, Mister Rabbit, you look mighty thin.
Yes, my Lawd, been cutting through the wind.
Refrain:

The Eency Weency Spider

Een - cy ween - cy spi - der went up the wa - ter spout,

Down came the rain_____ and washed the spi - der out,

Out came the sun_____ and dried up all the rain,

Now een - cy ween - cy spi - der went up the spout a - gain.

I Had a Little Rooster

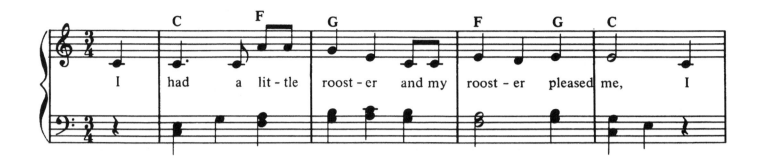

I had a lit - tle roost - er and my roost - er pleased me, I

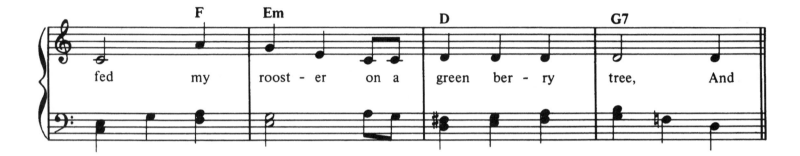

fed my roost - er on a green ber - ry tree, And

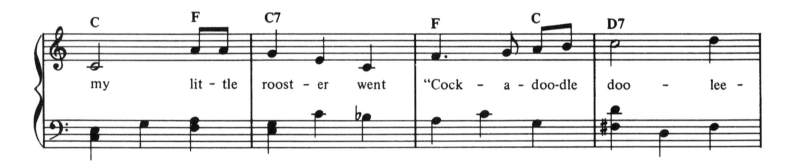

my lit - tle roost - er went "Cock - a - doo - dle doo - lee -

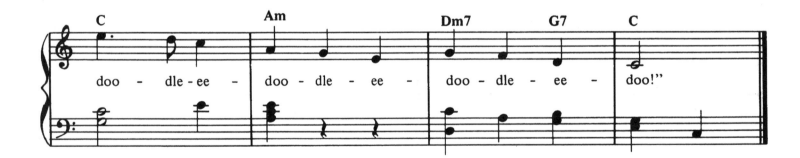

doo - dle - ee - doo - dle - ee - doo - dle - ee - doo!"

I had a little hen and my hen pleased me,
I fed my hen on a green berry tree,
And my little hen went "Cluck! Cluck! Cluck!"
And my little rooster went "Cock - a - doodle - doo - lee —
Doodle - ee - doodle - ee - doodle - ee - doo!"

I had a little duck, *(etc.)*
I fed my duck, *(etc.)*
And my little duck went "Quack! Quack! Quack!"
And my little hen went. *(etc.)*

The Old Gray Mare

Oh the old gray mare, She ain't what she used to be,

Ain't what she used to be, Ain't what she used to be, The

old gray mare, She ain't what she used to be

Man - y long years a - go.

Three Little Kittens

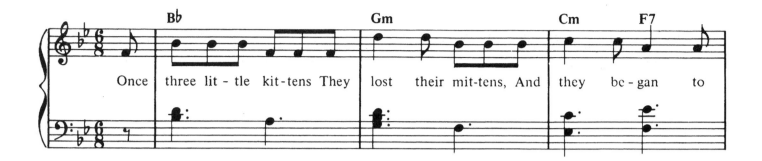

Once three lit - tle kit-tens They lost their mit-tens, And they be - gan to

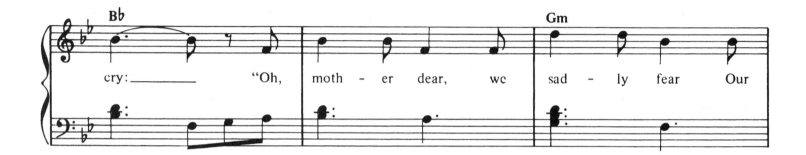

cry:_____ "Oh, moth - er dear, we sad - ly fear Our

mit - tens we have lost!"_____ "What! Lost your mit - tens! You

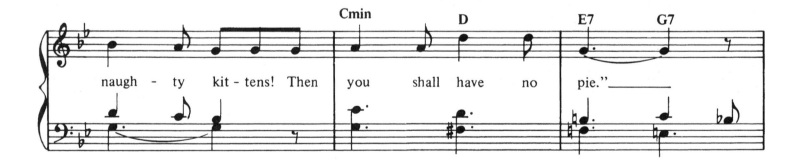

naugh - ty kit - tens! Then you shall have no pie."_____

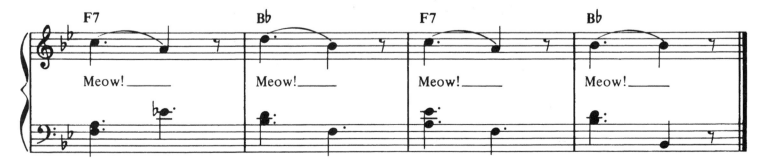

Meow!_____ Meow!_____ Meow!_____ Meow!_____

The three little kittens, they found their mittens,
And they began to cry:
"Oh, mother dear, see here, see here!
Our mittens we have found!"
"What! Found your mittens? You darling kittens!
Then you shall have some pie!"
"Meow! Meow! Meow! Meow!"

The three little kittens put on their mittens
And soon ate up the pie.
"Oh, mother dear, we greatly fear
Our mittens we have soiled."
"What! Soiled your mittens? You naughty kittens!"
Then they began to sigh,
"Meow! Meow! Meow! Meow!"

The three little kittens, they washed their mittens,
And hung them up to dry.
"Oh, mother dear, look here, look here!
Our mittens we have washed."
"What! Washed your mittens? You darling kittens!
But I smell a rat close by!
Hush! Hush! Hush! Hush!"

Hark! Hark! the Dogs Do Bark

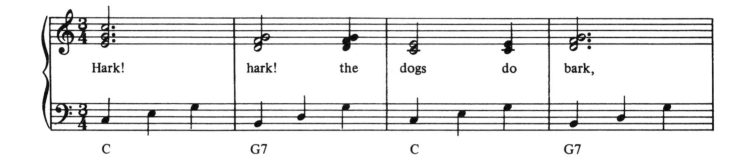

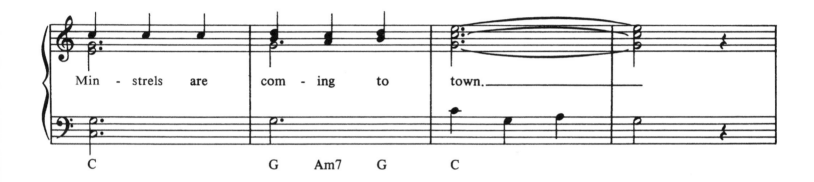

Hark! hark! the dogs do bark,

C · G7 · C · G7

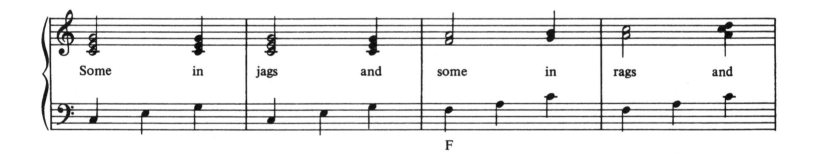

Min - strels are com - ing to town.

C · G · Am7 · G · C

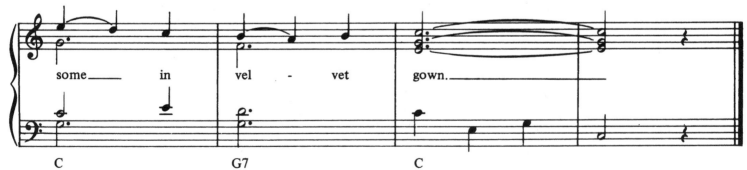

Some in jags and some in rags and

F

some in vel - vet gown.

C · G7 · C

Baa, Baa Black Sheep

Baa, Baa black sheep have you an-y wool?

C   F   C

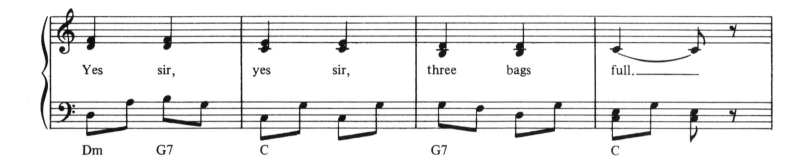

Yes sir, yes sir, three bags full.

Dm   G7   C   G7   C

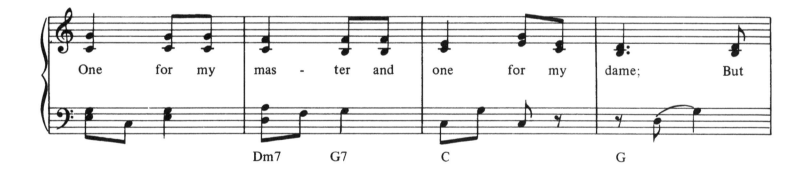

One for my mas - ter and one for my dame; But

Dm7   G7   C   G

none for the lit - tle boy that cries in the lane.

C   Dm7   C   G7   C

Pussy Cat, Pussy Cat

Pus-sy cat, pus-sy cat, where have you been? I've been to Lon-don to vis-it the Queen.

Pus-sy cat, pus-sy cat, what did you there? I frightened a lit-tle mouse un-der her chair.

Ladybird, Ladybird, Fly Away Home

Lad-y-bird, lad-y-bird, fly a-way home, your house is on fire and your child-ren have flown.

Two Little Dicky Birds

Two lit – tle dic – ky birds, sit – ting on a wall; ____

One named Pe – ter, one named Paul. ____

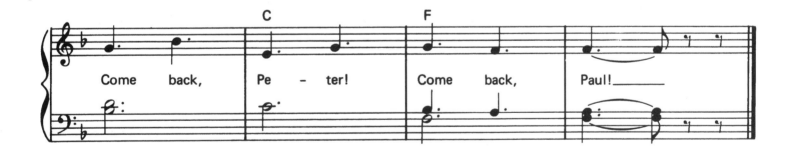

Fly a – way, Pe – ter! Fly a – way, Paul! ____

Come back, Pe – ter! Come back, Paul! ____

Two little dicky birds, sitting on a wall;
One named Peter, one named Paul.
Fly away, Peter! Fly away, Paul!
Come back, Peter! Come back, Paul!

Ride a Cock-Horse

Oh Where, Oh Where Has My Little Dog Gone?

Oh where, oh where has my lit - tle dog gone, Oh

G   D7

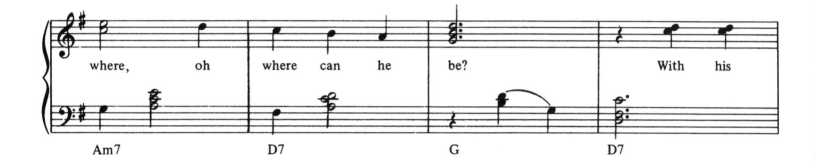

where, oh where can he be? With his

Am7   D7   G   D7

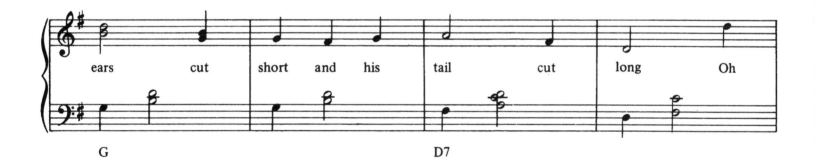

ears cut short and his tail cut long Oh

G   D7

where, oh where_____ is he?_____

Am7   D7   G   Am7   G

Froggy Went A-Courtin'

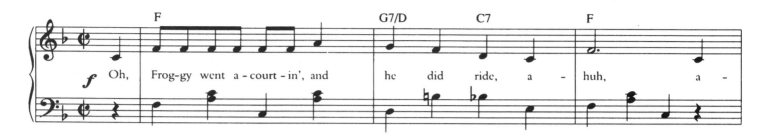

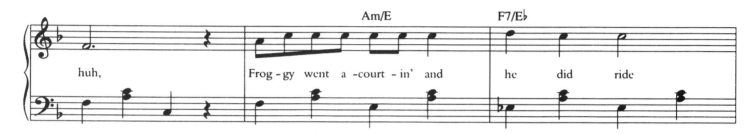

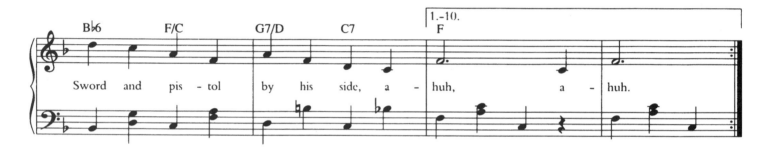

2. Well, he rode down to Miss Mouse's door, a-huh, a-huh,
   Well, he rode down to Miss Mouse's door,
   Where he had often been before, a-huh, a-huh.

3. He took Miss Mousie on his knee,*etc.*
   Said, "Miss Mousie will you marry me?"*etc.*

4. "I'll have to ask my Uncle Rat,"
   "See what he will say to that."

5. "Without my Uncle Rat's consent,"
   "I would not marry the President."

6. Well, Uncle Rat rode off to town,
   To buy his niece a wedding gown.

7. "Where will the wedding supper be?"
   "Way down yonder in a hollow tree."

8. "What will the wedding supper be?"
   "A fried mosquito and a roasted flea."

9. First to come in were two little ants,
   Fixing around to have a dance.

10. Next to come in was a bumblebee,
    Bouncing a fiddle on his knee.

11. And next to come was a big tomcat,
    He swallowed the frog and the mouse and the rat.

Glow Worm

Shine, lit-tle glow worm, glim - mer, glim - mer; Shine, lit-tle glow worm,

glim - mer, glim - mer. Lead us, lest too far we wan - der;

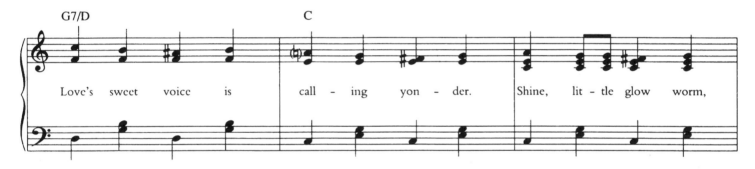

Love's sweet voice is call - ing yon - der. Shine, lit - tle glow worm,

glim - mer, glim - mer; Shine lit - tle glow worm, glim - mer. glim - mer.

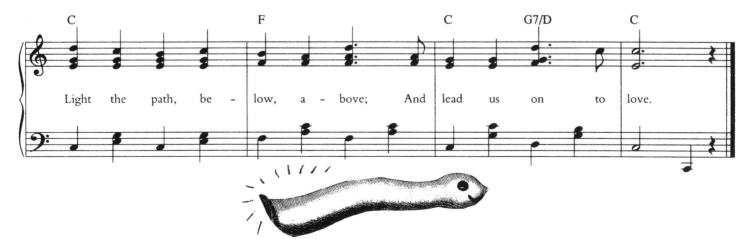

Light the path, be - low, a - bove; And lead us on to love.

The Bear Went over the Mountain

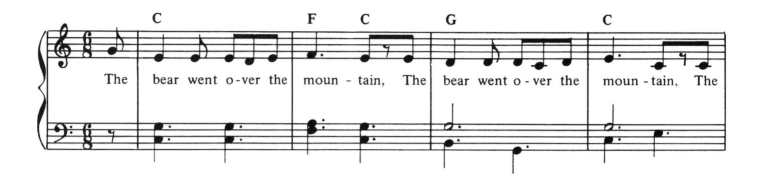

The bear went o-ver the moun-tain, The bear went o-ver the moun-tain, The

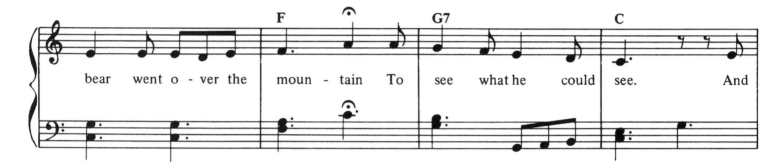

bear went o-ver the moun-tain To see what he could see. And

all that he could see, And all that he could see was The

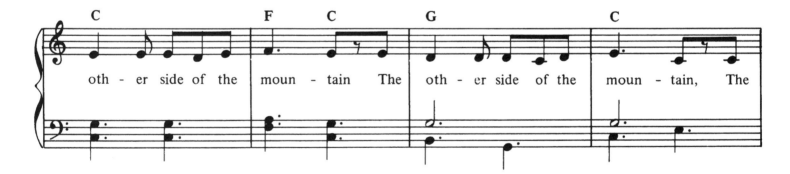

oth - er side of the moun-tain The oth - er side of the moun-tain, The

oth - er side of the moun-tain was all__ that he could see.

Little Robin Redbreast

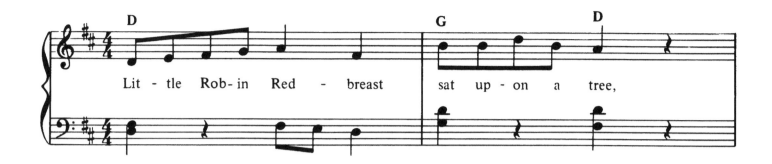

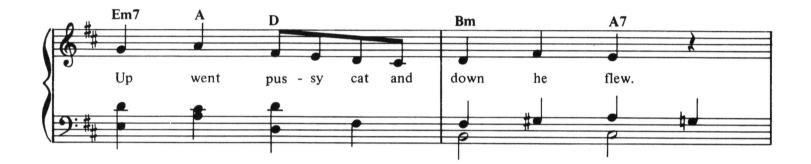

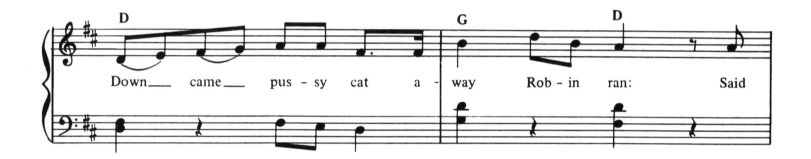

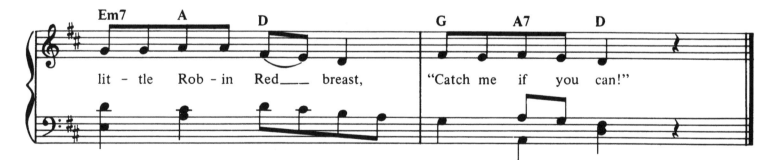

Little Robin Redbreast jumped upon a wall;
Pussycat jumped after him and almost had a fall;
Little Robin chirped and sang, and what did pussy say?
Pussycat said naught but, "Meow," and Robin flew away.

The Crawdad Song

1. You get a line and I'll get a pole, Ho-ney.
2. Here comes a man with a pack on his back, Ho-ney.

You get a line and I'll get a pole, Babe.
Here comes a man with a pack on his back, Babe.

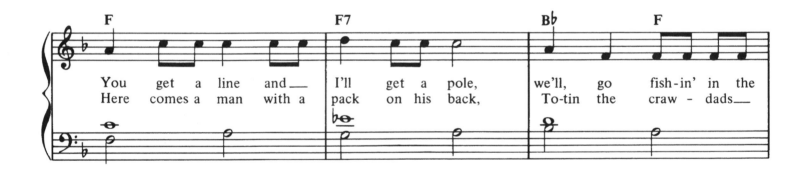

You get a line and I'll get a pole, we'll, go fish-in' in the
Here comes a man with a pack on his back, To-tin the craw - dads

craw-dad hole, Ho-ney, Oh Ba - by Mine.
in his pack,

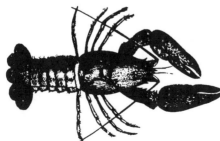

3. Whatcha gonna do when the stream runs dry, Honey,
Whatcha gonna do when the stream runs dry, Babe,
Whatcha gonna do when the stream runs dry,
Sit on the bank, watch the crawdads die,
Honey, Oh, Baby Mine.

I Love Little Pussy

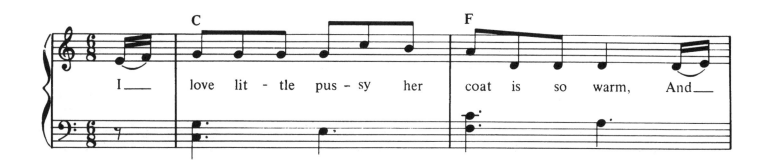

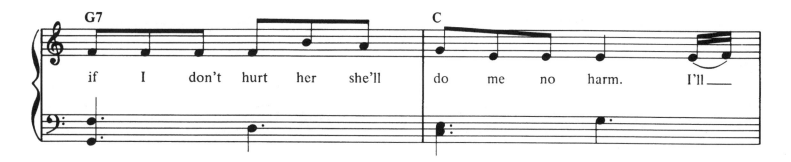

I love lit-tle pus-sy her coat is so warm, And if I don't hurt her she'll do me no harm. I'll

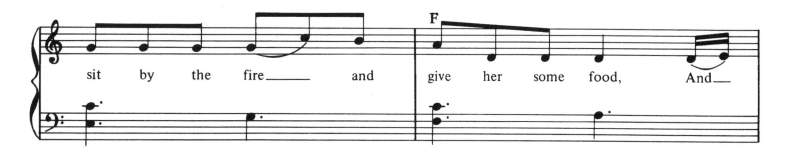

sit by the fire and give her some food, And

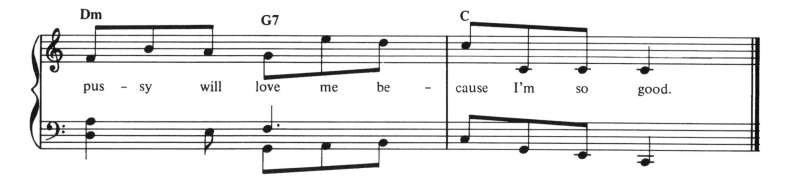

pus-sy will love me be-cause I'm so good.

This Little Pig Went to Market

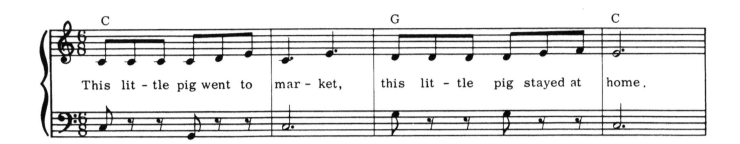

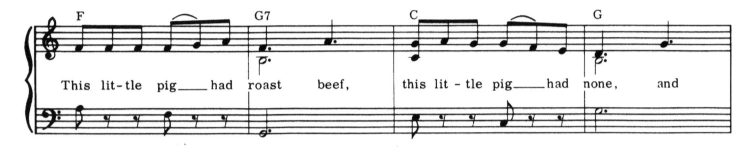

This lit-tle pig went to mar-ket, this lit-tle pig stayed at home.

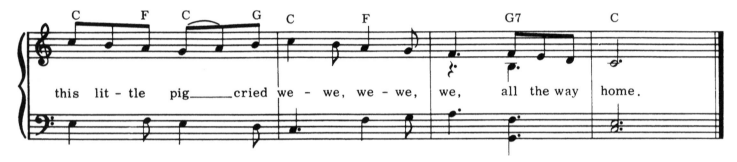

This lit-tle pig___ had roast beef, this lit-tle pig___ had none, and

this lit-tle pig___ cried we - we, we - we, we, all the way home.

Pop! Goes the Weasel

The Fox

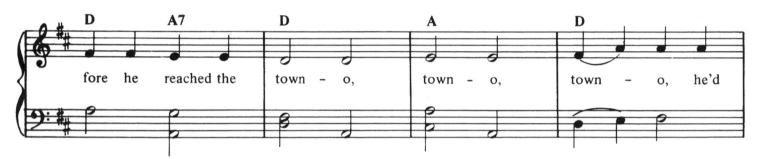

The fox went out on a chil-ly night, Prayed for the moon to give him light, For he'd ma-ny a mile to go that night be-fore he reached the town - o, town - o, town - o, he'd ma-ny a mile__ to go that night be - fore he reached the town - o.

He ran till he came to a great big bin
The ducks and the geese were lying within
Said, a couple of you will grease my chin
Before I leave this town - o, *etc.*

He grabbed the grey goose by the neck
Slung the little one over his back,
He didn't mind their quack - quack - quack
And the legs all dangling down - o, *etc.*

Old mother pitter - patter jumped out of bed
Out of the window she cocked her head
Crying, John, John, the grey goose is gone
And the fox is on the town - o, *etc.*

John, he went to the top of the hill
Blew his horn both loud and shrill;
The fox, he said, I'll flee with my kill
He'll soon be on my trail - o, *etc.*

He ran till he came to his cozy den
There were the little ones, eight, nine, ten,
They said daddy, you better go back again,
'Cause it must be a mighty fine town - o, *etc.*

Then the fox and his wife without any strife
Cut up the goose with fork and knife,
They never had such a supper in their life
And the little ones chewed on the bones - o, *etc.*

Five Fat Turkeys

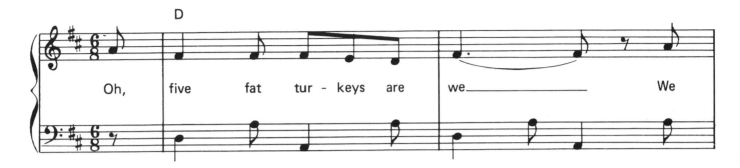

Oh, five fat tur-keys are we____ We

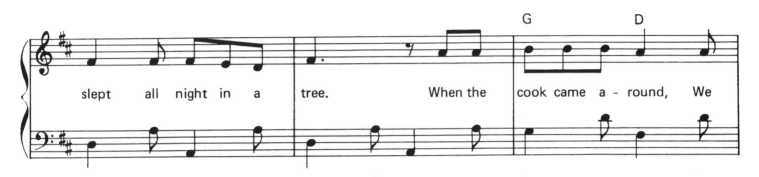

slept all night in a tree. When the cook came a-round, We

could-n't be found, And that's why we're here, You see.____

Old MacDonald Had a Farm

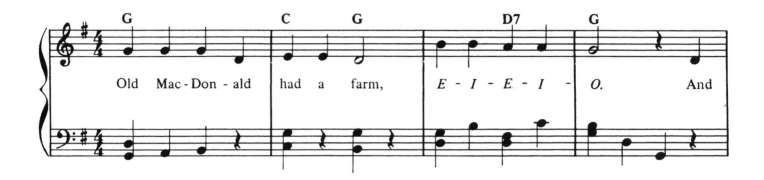

Old Mac-Don-ald had a farm, E - I - E - I - O. And

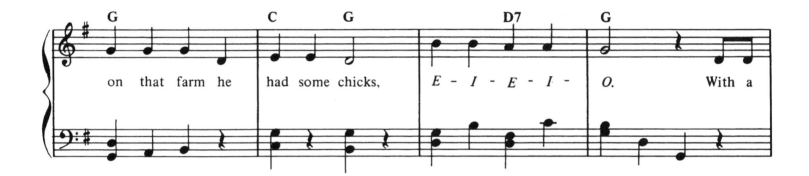

on that farm he had some chicks, E - I - E - I - O. With a

chick-chick here, and a chick-chick there, Here a chick, there a chick,

ev-'ry where a chick chick. Old Mac-Don-ald had a farm, E - I - E - I - O.

Old MacDonald had a farm,
E - I - E - I - O.
And on that farm he had some ducks,
E - I - E - I - O.
With a quack - quack here, and a quack - quack there,
Here a quack, there a quack, everywhere a quack - quack,
Chick - chick here, and a chick - chick there,
Here a chick, there a chick, everywhere a chick - chick.
Old MacDonald had a farm,
E - I - E - I - O.

. . . And on that farm he had some cows . . .
With a moo - moo here, and a moo - moo there,
Here a moo, there a moo, everywhere a moo - moo,
Quack - quack here and a quack - quack there . . .
Chick - chick here and a chick - chick there . . .

. . . And on that farm he had some pigs . .
With an oink - oink here, and an oink - oink there . . .
A moo - moo here . . .
Quack - quack here . . .
Chick - chick here . . .

. . . And on that farm he had some sheep . . .
With a baa - baa here, and a baa - baa there . . .

The Little Skunk

Oh I stuck my head in the lit - tle skunk's hole, And the

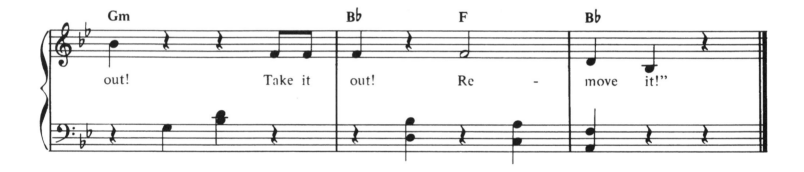

lit - tle skunk said, "Well bless my soul! Take it out! Take it

out! Take it out! Re - move it!"

Oh, I stuck my head in the little skunk's hole
And the little skunk said, "Well bless my soul!
Take it out! Take it out! Take it out! Remove it!"

Oh, I didn't take it out, and the little skunk said:
"If you don't take it out you'll wish you had.
Take it out! Take it out!" Pheeew! I removed it.

STORYBOOK SONGS

Little Boy Blue

Lit-tle Boy blue, come blow your horn, the sheep's in the mead-ow, the cow's in the corn.

Where's the boy who looks af-ter the sheep? He's un-der the hay-stack fast a-sleep.

Will you wak-en him? No, not I, for if I do,— he's sure to cry.

Simple Simon

Little Tommy Tucker

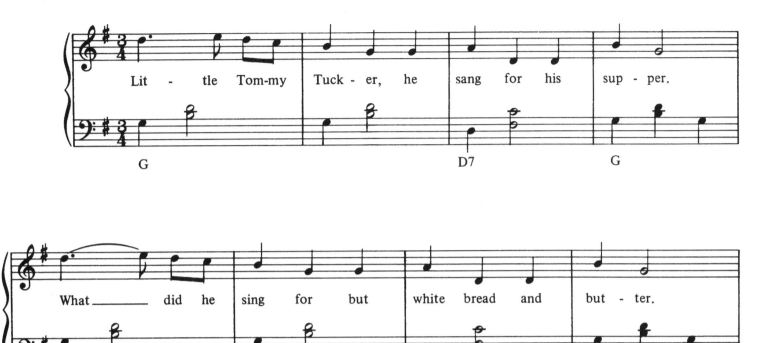

Lit - tle Tom-my Tuck - er, he sang for his sup - per.

G   D7   G

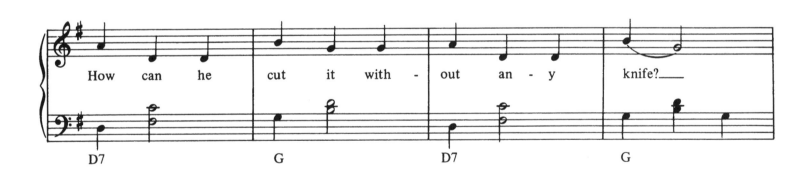

What ____ did he sing for but white bread and but - ter.

D7   G

How can he cut it with - out an - y knife? ____

D7   G   D7   G

How ____ can he mar - ry with - out an - y wife.

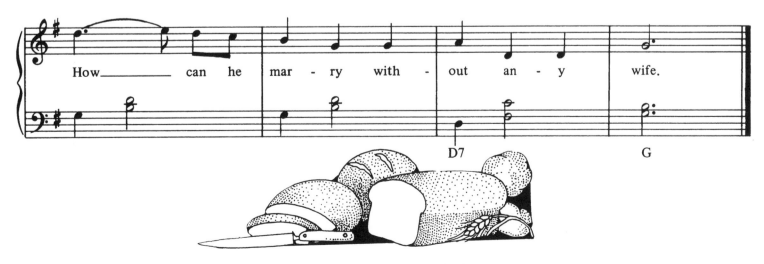

D7   G

Mary Had a Little Lamb

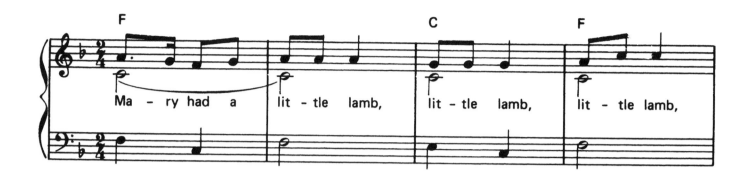

Ma – ry had a lit – tle lamb, lit – tle lamb, lit – tle lamb,

Ma – ry had a lit – tle lamb, its fleece was white as snow.

Handy Spandy

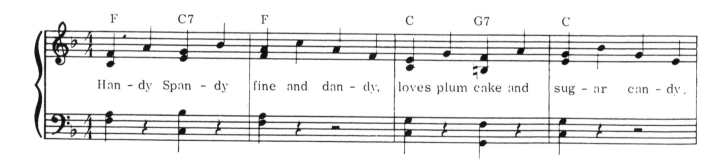

Han – dy Span – dy fine and dan – dy, loves plum cake and sug – ar can – dy.

Bought it from a can – dy shop, and a – way did hop, hop, hop.

Jack Spratt

Jack Spratt could eat no fat, His wife could eat no lean; and

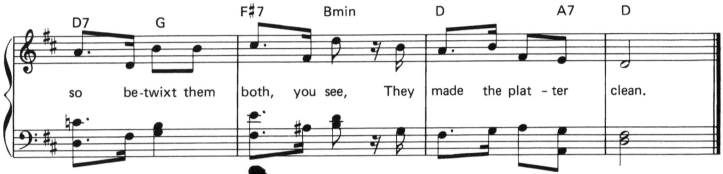

so be-twixt them both, you see, They made the plat-ter clean.

Humpty Dumpty

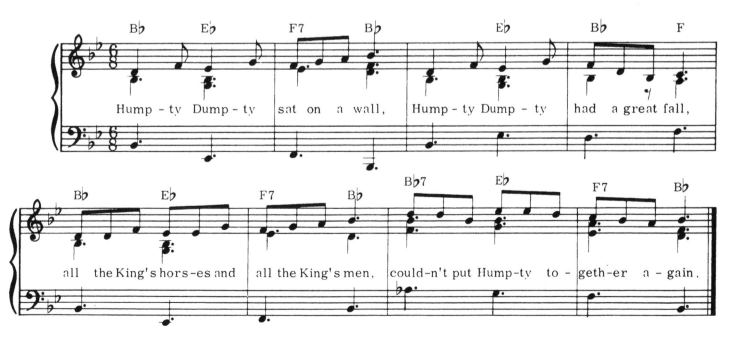

Hump-ty Dump-ty sat on a wall, Hump-ty Dump-ty had a great fall,

all the King's hors-es and all the King's men, could-n't put Hump-ty to-geth-er a-gain.

Lucy Locket

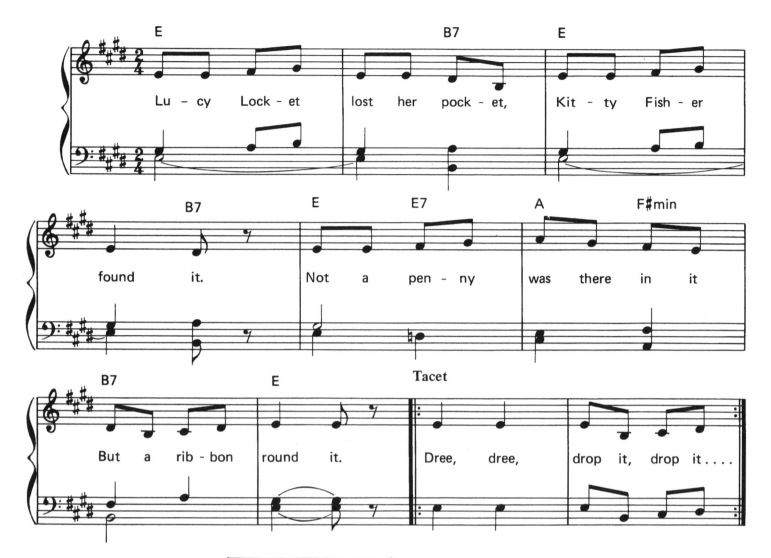

Lu – cy Lock – et lost her pock – et, Kit – ty Fish – er found it. Not a pen – ny was there in it But a rib – bon round it. Dree, dree, drop it, drop it....

Doctor Foster

Doc - tor Fos - ter went to Glouces-ter in a show - er of rain, _____ he
stepped in a pud - dle, right up to his mid-dle, and nev - er went there a - gain.

Little Jack Horner

Lit-tle Jack Hor - ner sat in the cor - ner, eat-ing a Christ - mas pie. He
put in his thumb, and pulled out a plum, and said, what a good boy am I.

The Muffin Man

Do you know the Muf-fin Man, the Muf-fin Man, the Muf-fin Man? Oh,

do you know the man, who sells his muf-fins on the street?

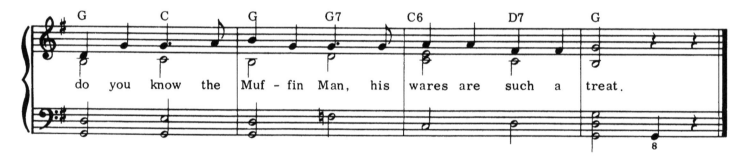

Do you know the Muf-fin Man, the Muf-fin Man, the Muf-fin Man? Oh,

do you know the Muf-fin Man, his wares are such a treat.

Wee Willie Winkie

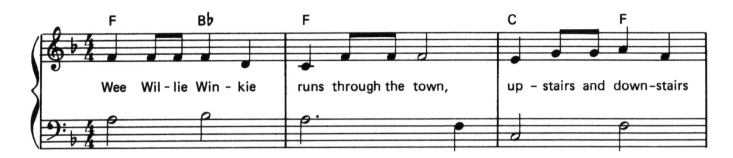
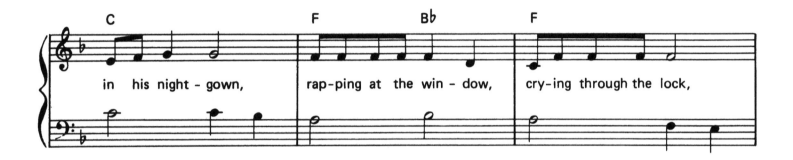
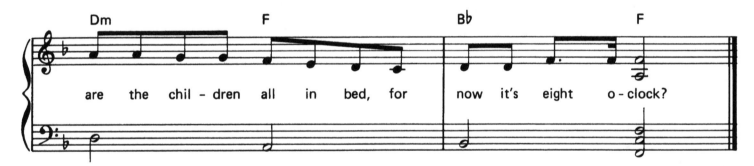

Little Miss Muffet

Lit - tle Miss Muf - fet sat on a tuf - fet,
eat - ing her curds and whey. There
came a great spi - der and sat down be - side her, which
fright - en'd Miss Muf - fet a - way.

Jack and Jill

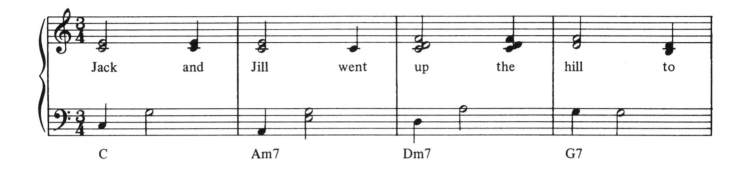

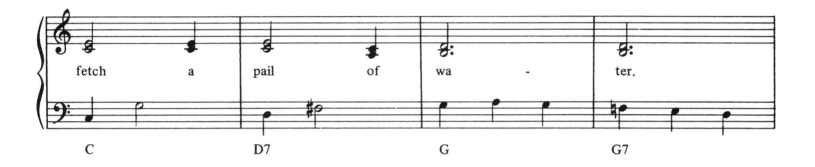

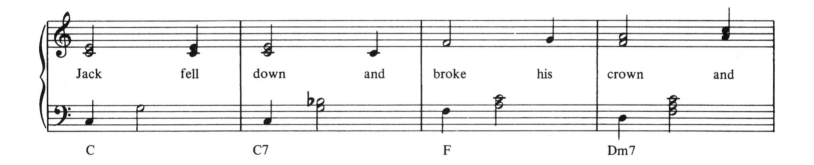

Old King Cole

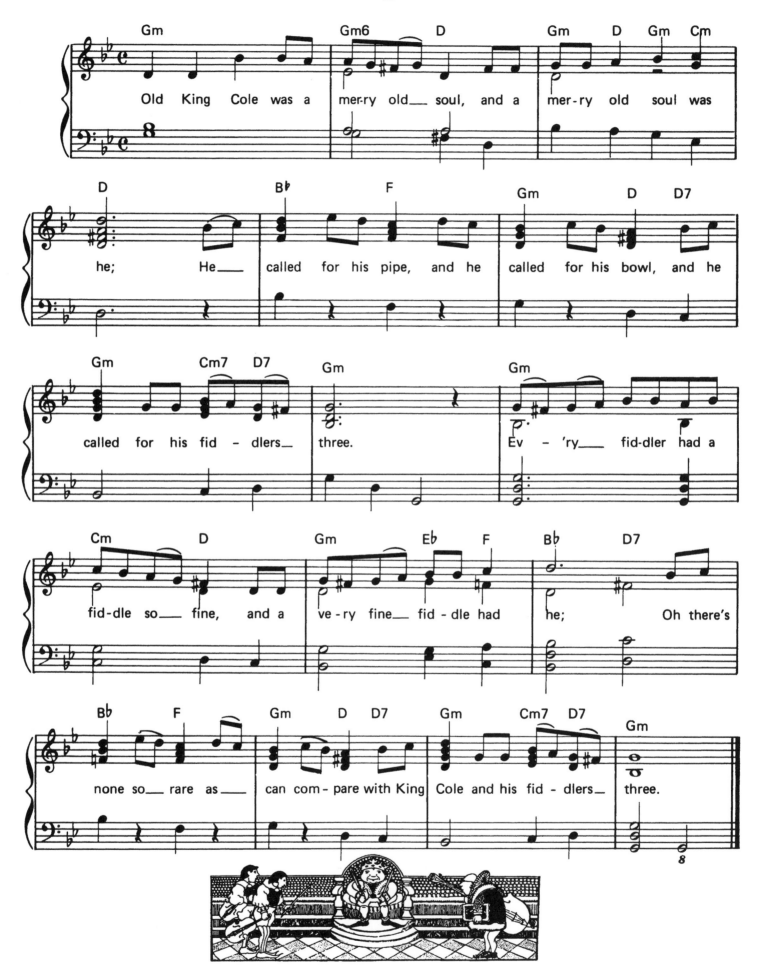

Old King Cole was a merry old___ soul, and a mer-ry old soul was he; He___ called for his pipe, and he called for his bowl, and he called for his fid - dlers___ three. Ev - 'ry___ fid-dler had a fid-dle so___ fine, and a ve-ry fine___ fid-dle had he; Oh there's none so___ rare as___ can com-pare with King Cole and his fid - dlers___ three.

Mary, Mary, Quite Contrary

Ma - ry, Ma - ry, quite con - trar - y, how does your gar - den grow? With

sil - ver bells and cock - le shells, and pret-ty maids all in a row.

Little Bopeep

Lit - tle Bo - peep has lost her sheep, and does-n't know where___to find them.

Leave them a - lone, and they'll___come home, bring-ing their tails ___ be - hind them.

COUNTING AND LEARNING

The Alphabet Song

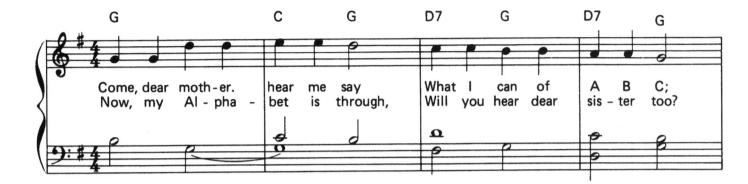

Come, dear moth-er. hear me say What I can of A B C;
Now, my Al-pha - bet is through, Will you hear dear sis – ter too?

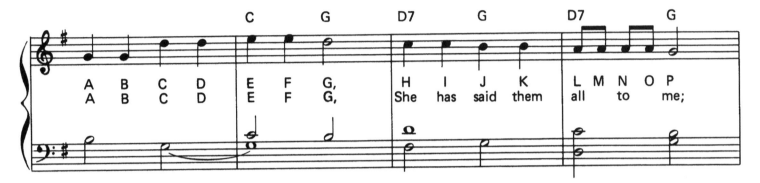

A B C D E F G, H I J K L M N O P
A B C D E F G, She has said them all to me;

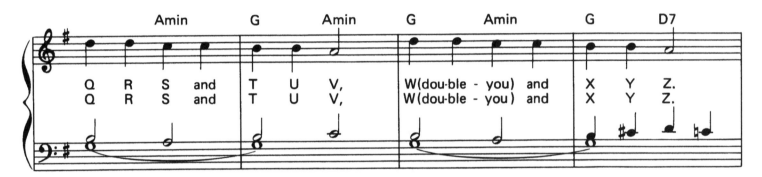

Q R S and T U V, W(dou-ble - you) and X Y Z.
Q R S and T U V, W(dou-ble - you) and X Y Z.

Now you've heard my A B C, Tell me what you think of me.
Now we've said our A B C, Let us have a kiss from thee.

This Old Man

This old man, he played two . . . shoe, etc.

This old man, he played three . . . knee, etc.

Four . . . floor, etc.

Five . . . hive, etc.

Six . . . sticks, etc.

Seven . . . up in heaven, etc.

Eight . . . at my gate, etc.

Nine . . . on my spine, etc.

Ten . . . once again, etc.

The Seasons

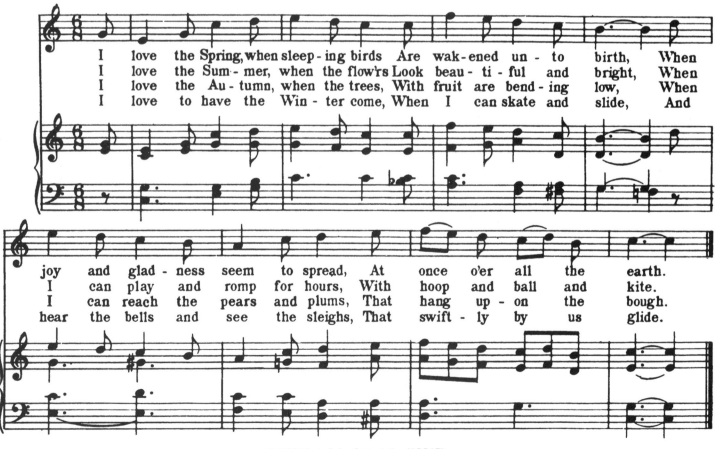

B-I-N-G-O

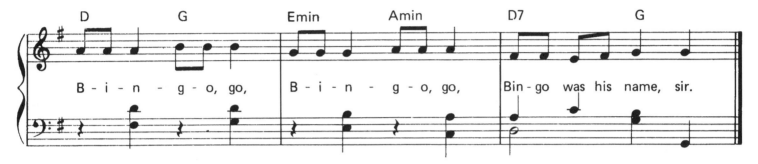

Johnny had a little dog, And Bingo was his name, sir, B-i-n-g-o, go,

B-i-n-g-o, go, B-i-n-g-o, go, Bingo was his name, sir.

One Finger, One Thumb, One Hand

One fin-ger, one thumb, one hand_____ keep mov - ing,_____ One

fin-ger, one thumb, one hand__ keep mov - ing,___ One fin-ger, one thumb, one hand,__ keep

mov - ing, And we'll all be hap - py and gay!

There Were Ten in the Bed

There were ten in the bed and the lit - tle one said: "Roll o - ver,___ roll o - ver!"___ So they all rolled o - ver and one fell out.___

There were nine in the bed and the little one said, etc.
There were eight in the, etc.
There were seven in the, etc.
There were six in the, etc.
There were five in the, etc.
There were four in the, etc.
There were three in the, etc.
There were two in the, etc.
There was one in the bed and the little one said *GOOD NIGHT*

One, Two, Buckle My Shoe

One, Two, Buck-le My Shoe, Three, four, O-pen the door, Five, six,

Pick up sticks, sev-en, eight, Lay them straight, Nine, ten, A good fat hen,

E-lev-en, twelve, Dig and delve, Thir-teen, four-teen, Maids a-court-ing, Fif-teen, six-teen,

Maids in the kitch-en, Sev-en-teen, eight-een, Maids a-wait-ing, Nine-teen, twen-ty, My plate's emp-ty!

A, B, C, Tumble Down D

A, B, C, Tum-ble Down D, The cat's in the cup-board and can't see me.

Little Things

Lit - tle drops of wa - ter, Lit - tle grains of sand, Make the might - y
And the lit - tle mo - ments, Hum - ble though they be, Make the might - y

o - cean And the beau - teous land, And the beau - teous land.
a - ges Of e - ter - ni - ty, Of e - ter - ni - ty.

The Ants Came Marching

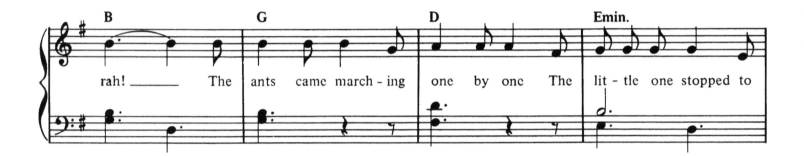

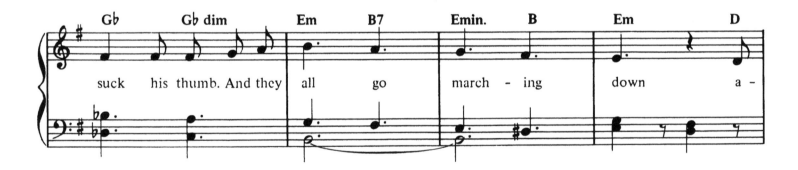

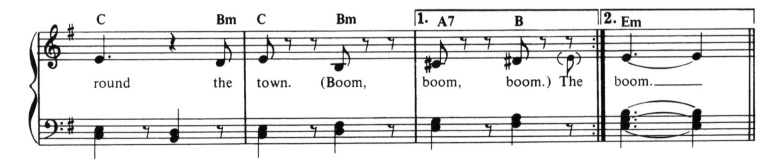

The ants came marching two by two, Hurrah! Hurrah!
The ants came marching two by two
The little one stopped to tie his shoe.
They all go marching down around the town.
(Boom, boom, boom.)

The ants came marching three by three . . .
The little one stopped to climb a tree.

The ants came marching four by four . . .
The little one stopped to shut the door . . .

The ants came marching five by five . . .
The little one stopped to take a dive . . .

The ants came marching six by six . . .
The little one stopped to pick up sticks . . .

The ants came marching seven by seven. . .
The little one stopped to go to heaven . . .

The ants came marching eight by eight . . .
The little one stopped to shut the gate . . .

The ants came marching nine by nine . . .
The little one stopped to scratch his spine.

The ants came marching ten by ten . . .
The little one stopped to say *The end.*

Oats, Peas, Beans and Barley Grow

Oats, Peas, Beans And Bar - ley Grow, Oats, Peas, Beans And Bar - ley Grow, Can
Thus the farm - er sows his seed, Thus he stands and takes his ease,

you or I or an - y - one know, How Oats, Peas, Beans And Bar - ley Grow.
Stamps his foot and clasps his hands, And turns a - round and views the land.

Wait - ing for a part - ner, Wait - ing for a part - ner,
Tra, la, la, la, la, la,

O - pen the ring and choose one in while we all gai - ly dance and sing.
Tra, la, la, la, la, la, la, la, Tra, la, la, la, la, la, la, la.

Five Little Monkeys

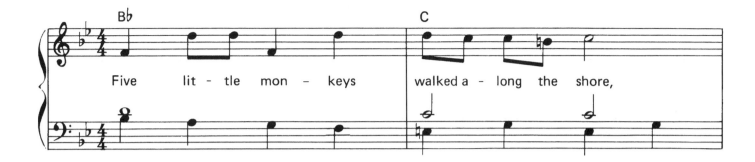

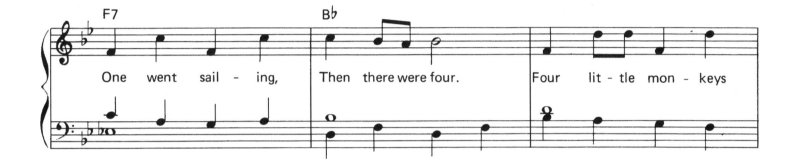

Three little monkeys found a pot of glue,
One got stuck in it,
Then there were two.

Two little monkeys found a raisin bun,
One ran away with it,
Then there was one.

One little monkey, red in the face,
They trained him as an astronaut
And sent him out in space.

Six Little Ducks

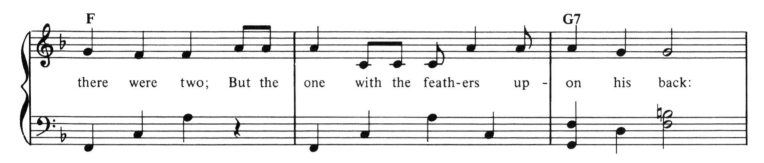

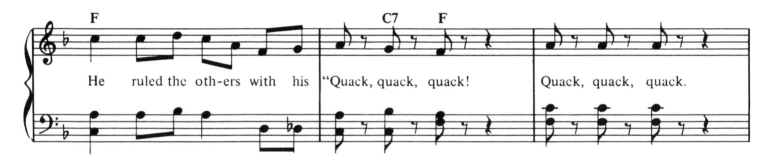

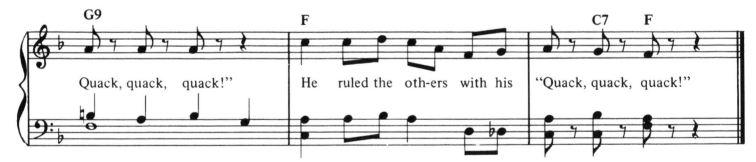

2. Down to the water they would go,
    Wibble - wobble, wibble wobble, to and fro,
    But the one with the feathers upon his back:
    He ruled the others with his "Quack quack quack! Quack quack quack!"
    He ruled the others with his "Quack quack quack!"

3. Home from the water they would come
    Wibble - wobble, wibble - wobble, ho ho hum!
    But the one with the feathers upon his back:
    He ruled the others with his "Quack quack quack! Quack quack quack!"
    He ruled the others with his "Quack quack quack!"

One, Two, Three, Four, Five

One, two, three, four, five, Once I caught a fish a—live,

F   C⁷   F   C   F   Gm

Six, seven, eight, nine, ten, Then I let it go a—gain.

Gm   C⁷   Gm⁷   C⁷   F

Why did you let it go?
Because it bit my finger so.
Which finger did it bite?
This little finger on the right.

Ten Little Sailors

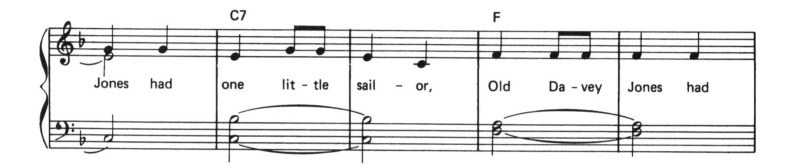

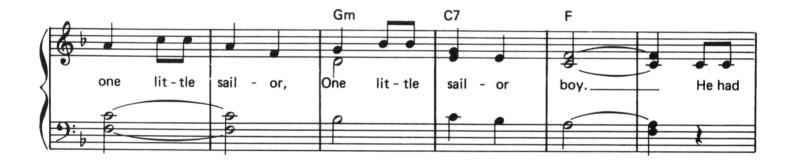

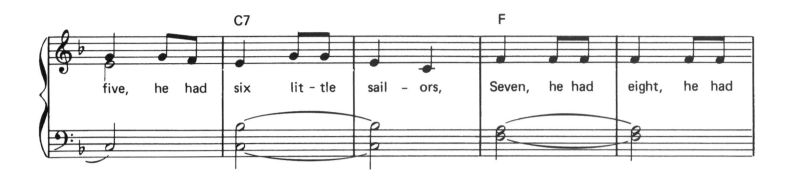

five, he had six lit - tle sail - ors, Seven, he had eight, he had

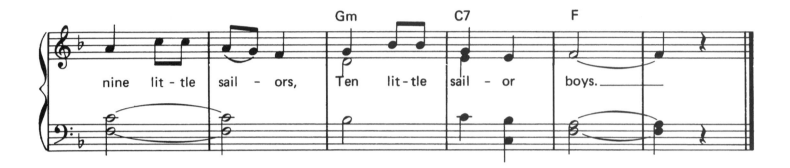

nine lit - tle sail - ors, Ten lit - tle sail - or boys.

Old Davey Jones had ten little sailors . . .

He had ten, he had nine, he had eight little sailors,
Seven little, six little, five little sailors,
Four little, three little, two little sailors,
One little sailor boy.

The Orchestra

I. The vi-o-lin's ring-ing like joy - - - ful -

II. The clar-i-net, the clar-i-net sings dood-le, dood-le, dood-le,

III. The trum-pet is sound-ing ta ta ta ta ta ta ta, ta ta ta

IV. The horn, the horn whose soug is for -

V. The drum plays on two tones and drones on the

Moderately

PIANO

mf

This old German Quodlibet is most effective when sung as a cumulative song as follows: (1) violin alone, (2) clarinet alone, (3) violin and clarinet together, (4) trumpet alone, (5) violin, clarinet and trumpet, (6) horn alone, (7) violin, clarinet, trumpet and horn, (8) drums alone, (9) all instruments together. Sing through twice, ritard on the end the second time. Group may be divided into five equal groups regardless of voices. It is fun to imitate playing the various instruments.

sing - ing, The vi - o - lin's ring - ing like joy - ful song.

doodle, det, The clar - i - net, the clar - i - net makes dood - le dood - le dood - le det.

ta ta ta ta, The trum - pet is sound - ing ta ta ta ta ta ta, ta ta ta ta.

lorn, The horn, the horn whose song is for - lorn.

same tones, Five one, one five, boom boom boom boom boom.

C   G7   C

The Calendar Song

Sixty seconds make a minute, Something sure you can learn in it;
Fifty-two weeks make a year, Soon a new one will be here;
Twenty-eight is all his share, With twenty nine in each leap year;

Sixty minutes make an hour, Work with all your might and pow'r,
Twelve long months a year will make, Say them now without mistake,
That you may the Leap-year know, Divide by four and that will show,

Twenty-four hours make a day, Time enough for work and play,
Thirty days hath gay September, April, June and cold November;
In each year are seasons four, You will learn them I am sure;

Seven days a week will make; You will learn if pains you take.
All the rest have thirty-one; Febuary stands alone.
Spring and Summer, then the Fall; Winter, last, but best of all.

PLAYTIME AND DANCE-AROUND

The Hokey Pokey

You put your right hand in, You put your right hand

out, You put your right hand in, And you shake it all a-

Chorus:

bout. You do the ho - key po - key And you turn your-self a-

round. That's what it's all a - bout. *Hey!*

You put your left hand in, etc.
Chorus

You put your right foot in, etc.
Chorus

You put your left foot in, etc.
Chorus

You put your big head in, etc.
Chorus

You put your backside in, etc.
Chorus

You put your whole self in, etc.
Chorus

Pat-a-Cake

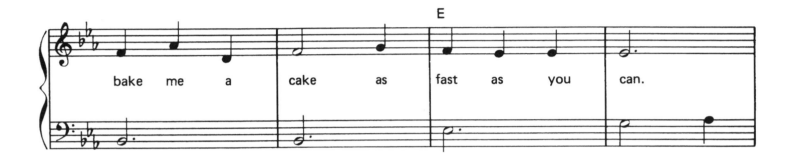

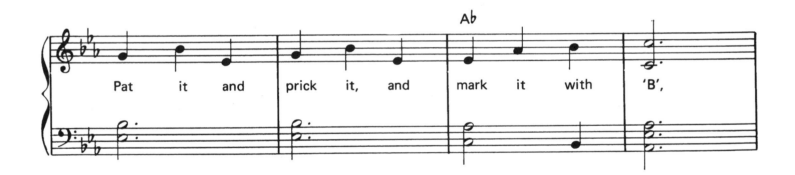

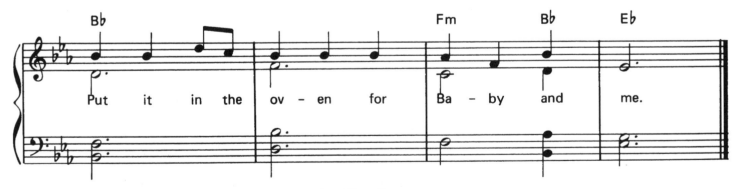

Polly Put the Kettle On

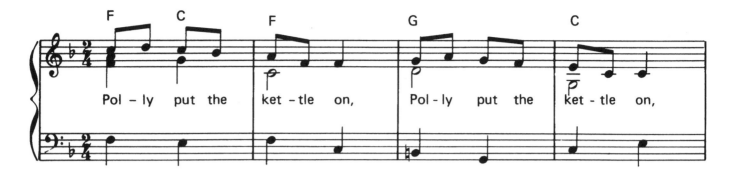

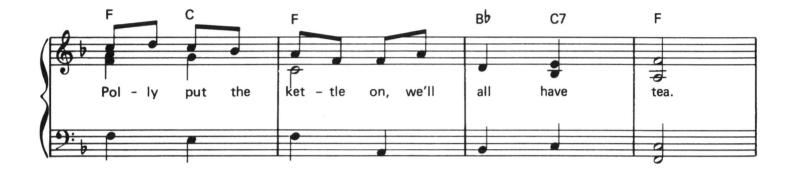

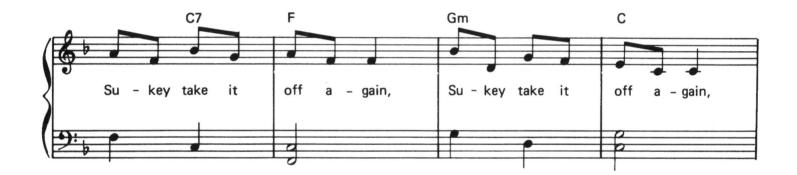

She'll Be Comin' 'Round the Mountain

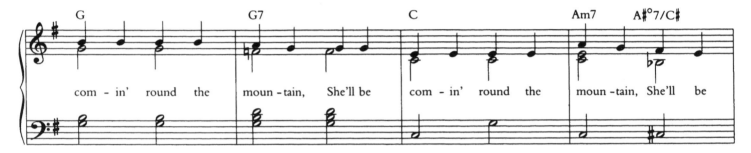

2. She'll be drivin' six white horses when she comes, *etc.*

3. Oh, we'll all go out to meet her when she comes, *etc.*

4. We will kill the old red rooster when she comes, *etc.*

5. We will all have chicken and dumplings when she comes, *etc.*

A-Tisket, A-Tasket

A - tis - ket, a - tas - ket, ___ A green and yel - low bas - ket; ___ I

bought a bas - ket for my love, And on the way I dropped ___ it. ___ I

dropped it, I dropped it, ___ Yes, on the way I dropped it; ___ A

lit - tle girl - ie picked it up, And took it to her love.

The North Wind Doth Blow

The North wind doth blow, And we shall have snow, And what will poor rob-in do then? He'll sit in the barn, And keep him-self warm, And tuck his head un-der his wing, poor thing!

What Care We?

What care we for gold or sil - ver? What care we for house or land? What care we for ships on the o - cean? On-ward go - ing hand in hand.

The King of France

The King of France with for-ty thous-and men, Rode up the hill and then rode down a-gain.
The King of France with for-ty thous-and men, Gave a sa-lute and then rode down a-gain.

Turn Again, Whittington

Turn a-gain Whit-ting-ton, thou worth-y cit-iz-en, Lord Mayor of Lon-don.

Ring-a-Ring o' Roses

A - ring-a-ring o' ro - ses, a pock-et full of pos - ies. A-
tish - oo! A-tish - oo! We all fall down.

Skip to My Lou

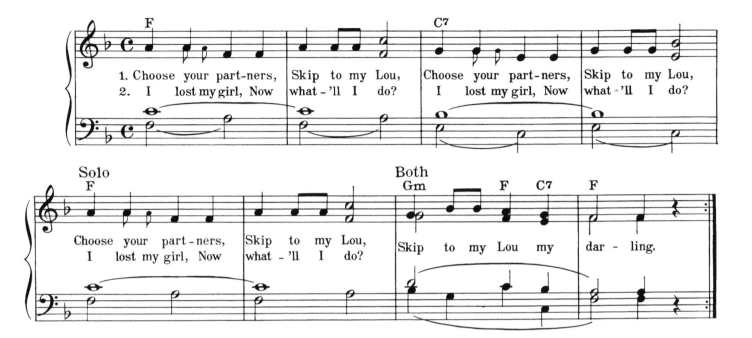

1. Choose your part-ners, Skip to my Lou, what-'ll I do?
2. I lost my girl, Now

Choose your part-ners, I lost my girl, Now

Skip to my Lou, what-'ll I do?

Solo

Choose your part-ners, I lost my girl, Now

Skip to my Lou, what-'ll I do?

Both

Skip to my Lou my dar-ling.

3. I'll get another, a sweeter one too;
4. Can't get a red bird, a blue bird'll do,
5. I got a red bird, a pretty one too,
6. Cat's in the cream jar, what'll I do?
7. Chicken in the dough tray, what'll I do?
8. Fly's in the buttermilk, shoo, shoo, shoo!
9. Pickles are sour, and so are you,
10. Hurry up slowpoke, do, oh, do!
11. My girl wears a number nine shoe,
12. Bears in the rose-bush, boo, boo, boo!
13. Cows in the stable, moo, moo, moo!
14. Come on big foot, what you goin' to do?

Ta-Ra-Ra Boom-De-Ay

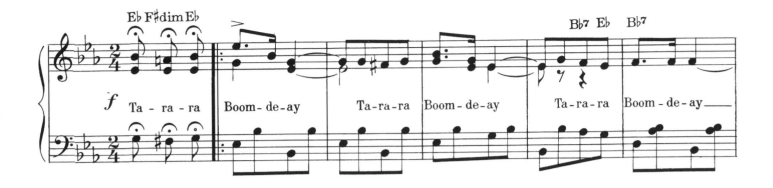

Oh Dear! What Can the Matter Be?

Oh Dear! What can the mat-ter be? Dear dear! What can the mat-ter be?

Oh Dear! What can the mat-ter be? John-ny's so long at the

fair.____ He prom-ised to buy me a bunch of blue rib-bons, he

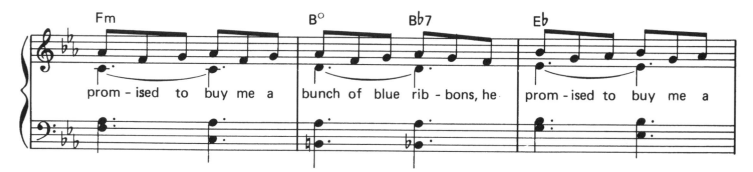

prom-ised to buy me a bunch of blue rib-bons, he prom-ised to buy me a

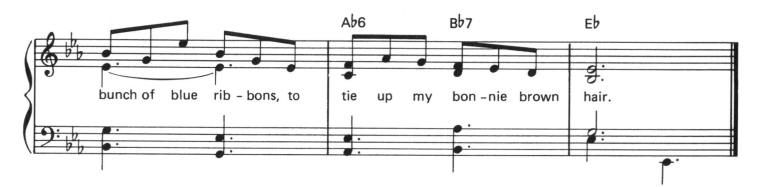

bunch of blue rib-bons, to tie up my bon-nie brown hair.

Looby Loo

Here we go Loo - by Loo,_____ Here we go Loo - by Light,_____
Put your right foot in,_____ Put your right foot out,_____

Here we go Loo - by Loo,_____ All on a Sat - ur - day night._____
Shake it a lit - tle, a lit - tle, And turn your-self a - bout._____

2. Here we go Looby Loo, *etc.*
   Put your left foot in, *etc.*

3. Here we go Looby Loo, *etc.*
   Put your right hand in, *etc.*

4. Here we go Looby Loo, *etc.*
   Put your left hand in, *etc.*

5. Here we go Looby Loo, *etc.*
   Put your noses in, *etc.*

6. Here we go Looby Loo, *etc.*
   Put your whole selves, *etc.*

Here We Go Round the Mulberry Bush

Here we go round the mul-ber-ry bush, the mul-ber-ry bush, the mul-ber-ry bush.

Here we go round the mul-ber-ry bush, on a cold and frost-y morn-ing.

See-Saw, Margery Daw

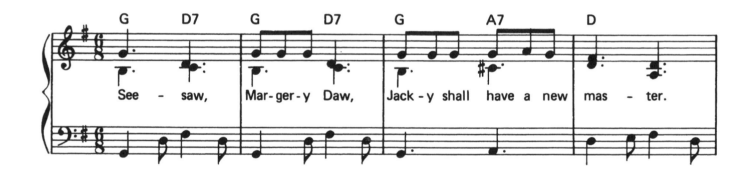

See - saw, Mar-ger-y Daw, Jack-y shall have a new mas - ter.

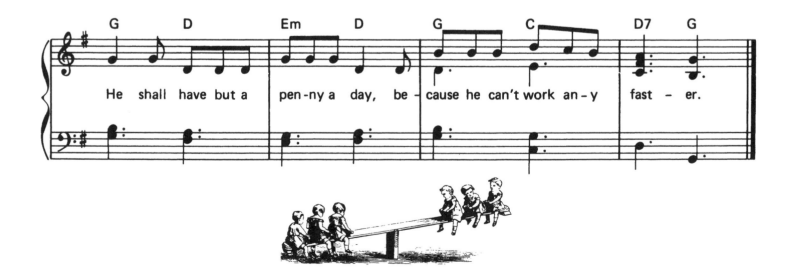

He shall have but a pen-ny a day, be - cause he can't work an-y fast - er.

The Grand Old Duke of York

Oh, the grand old Duke of York, he had ten thous-and men, he marched them up to the top of the hill and he marched them down a - gain. And when they were up, they were up, and when they were down, they were down, and when they were on - ly half - way up, they were neith - er up nor down.

Peek-a-Boo

Peek - a - boo, Peek - a - boo, Come from be - hind the chair so

Peek - a - boo, Peek - a - boo, I see you hid - ing there.___

The Farmer in the Dell

G

1. The farm - er in the dell, The farm - er in the dell,

Emin   G   D7   G

Heigh - o! the der - ry oh, The farm - er in the dell.

2. The farmer takes a wife, etc.
3. The wife takes the child, etc.
4. The child takes the nurse, etc.
5. The nurse takes the dog, etc.

6. The dog takes the cat, etc.
7. The cat takes the rat, etc.
8. The rat takes the cheese, etc.
9. The cheese stands alone, etc.

Brother, Come and Dance with Me

Broth-er, come and dance with me, Both my hands I'm of-f'ring thee, First this way,

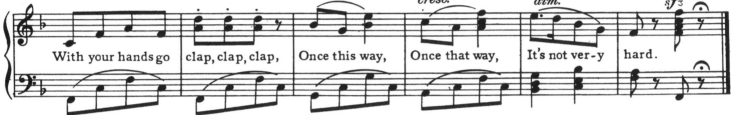

then that way, Then a-round, it is-n't hard. Now with your foot, go tap, tap, tap,

With your hands go clap, clap, clap, Once this way, Once that way, It's not ver-y hard.

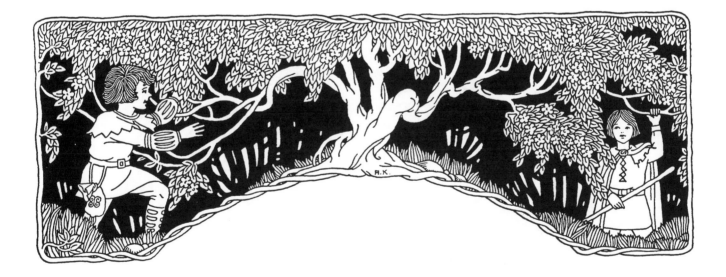

Girls and Boys Come Out to Play

Girls and boys come out to play, the moon is shin-ing bright as day.

C G7 C F G7 C Dm7

Leave your sup-per and leave your sleep and join your play-fel-lows in the street.

C G7 C F G7 C

SILLY SONGS

Knicky, Knicky, Knacky Noo

Put my hand on my-self, what have I here?

This is my head knock-er, my sou - ven-ir. Head knock-er, head knock-er,

knick-y, knick-y, knack-y noo; That's what they taught me when I went to school.

Put my hand on myself, what have I here?
This is my nose wiper . . .

This is my tea strainer . . .

This is my chin chopper . . .

This is my chest bumper . . .

This is my bread basket . . .

This is my thigh bumper . . .

This is my knee knocker . . .

This is my toe tapper . . .

This is my heel wagger . . .

Do Your Ears Hang Low?

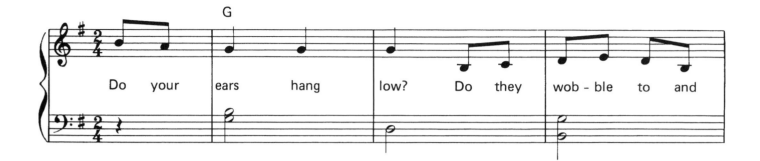

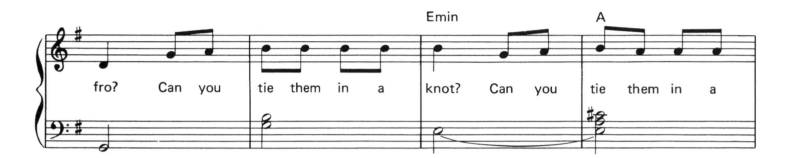

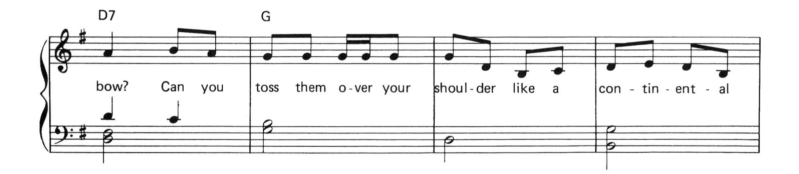

Do your ears hang low?
Do they wobble to and fro?
Can you tie them in a knot?
Can you tie them in a bow?
Can you toss them over your shoulder
Like a continental soldier?
Do your ears - hang - low?

Yes, my ears hang low.
They can wobble to and fro,
I can tie them in a knot,
I can tie them in a bow,
I can toss them over my shoulder
Like a continental soldier.
Yes, my ears - hang - low.

Fiddle-De-Dee

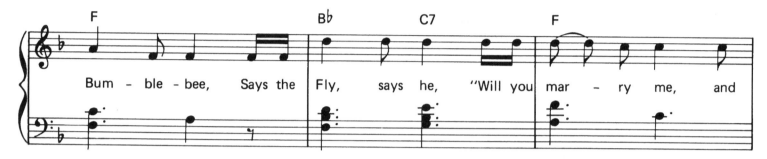

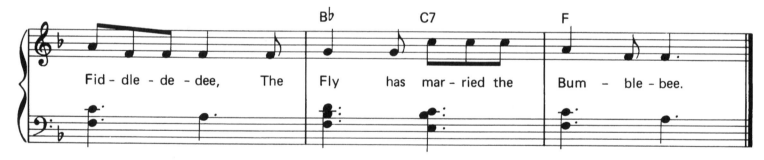

Fiddle - de - dee, fiddle - de - dee,
The Fly has married the Bumblebee.
Says the Fly, says he, "Will you marry me
And live with me, sweet Bumblebee?"
Fiddle - de - dee, fiddle - de - dee,
The Fly has married the Bumblebee.

Fiddle - de - dee, etc.
Says the Bee, says she, "I'll live under your wing,
And you'll never know I carry a sting."
Fiddle - de - dee, etc.

Fiddle - de - dee, etc.
And when Parson Beetle had married the pair,
They both went out to take the air;
Fiddle - de - dee, etc.

The Paw-Paw Patch

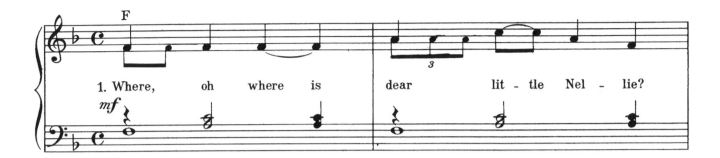

1. Where, oh where is dear lit – tle Nel – lie?

Where, oh where is dear lit – tle Nel – lie? Where, oh where is

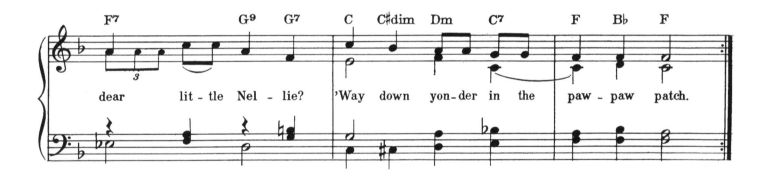

dear lit – tle Nel – lie? 'Way down yon-der in the paw – paw patch.

2. Come on, boys let's go find her,
   Come on, boys let's go find her,
   Come on, boys let's go find her,
   'Way down yonder in the paw-paw patch.

3. Pick-in' up paw-paws, puttin' 'em in your pocket,
   Pick-in' up paw paws, puttin' 'em in your pocket,
   Pick-in' up paw paws, puttin' 'em in your pocket,
   'Way down yonder in the paw-paw patch.

Aiken Drum

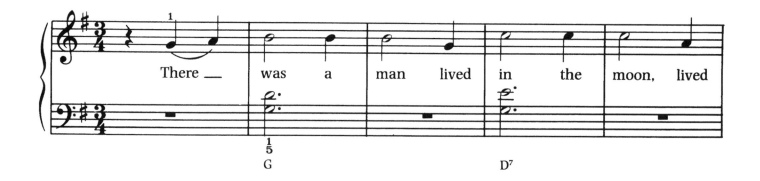

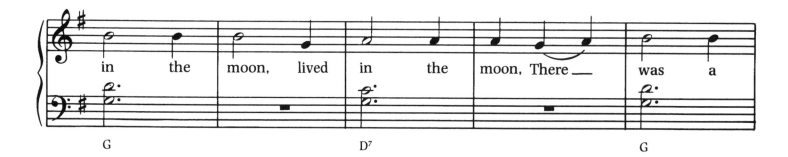

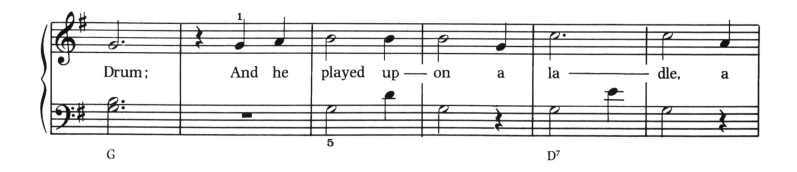

la ———— dle, a la ———— dle, And he played up—

G   D⁷   G

—on a la ———— dle, And his name was Ai—ken Drum.

G   D⁷   G   D⁷   G

And his hat was made of good cream cheese, . . .
And his name was Aiken Drum;
    And he played . . .

And his coat was made of good roast beef, . . .
And his name was Aiken Drum;
    And he played . . .

And his buttons were made of penny loaves, . . .
And his name was Aiken Drum;
    And he played . . .

His waistcoat was made of crust of pies, . . .
And his name was Aiken Drum;
    And he played . . .

Sing a Song of Sixpence

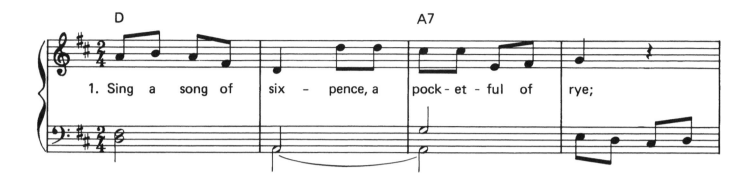

1. Sing a song of six - pence, a pock - et - ful of rye;

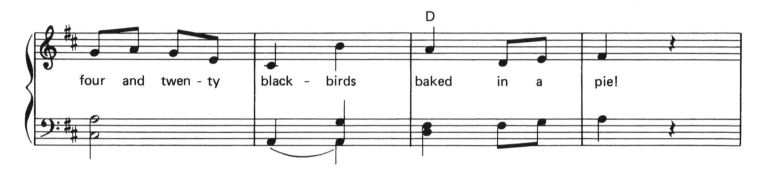

four and twen - ty black - birds baked in a pie!

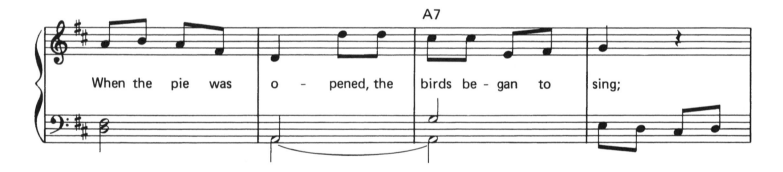

When the pie was o - pened, the birds be - gan to sing;

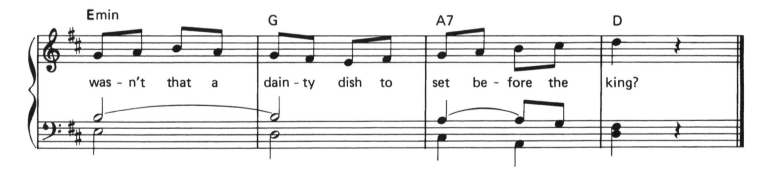

was - n't that a dain - ty dish to set be - fore the king?

2. The king was in his counting house,
   Counting out his money.
   The queen was in the parlor,
   Eating bread and honey.
   The maid was in the garden,
   Hanging out the clothes,
   When down came a blackbird
   And snipped off her nose!

Michael Finnegan

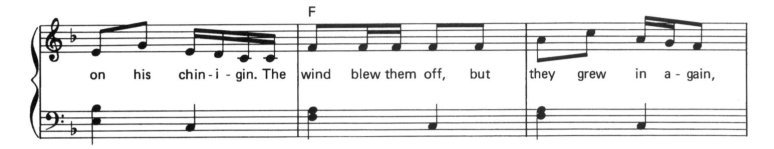

I know a man named Michael Finnegan.
He went fishing with a pin - agin,
Caught a fish and dropped it in - agin,
Poor old Michael Finnegan (begin again) . . . .

I know a man named Michael Finnegan.
Climbed a tree and barked his shin - agin,
Took off several yards of skin - igin,
Poor old Michael Finnegan (begin again) . . . .

I know a man named Michael Finnegan.
He kicked up an awful din - igin,
Because they said he could not sing - igin,
Poor old Michael Finnegan (begin again) . . . .

I know a man named Michael Finnegan.
He got fat and then got thin again,
Then he died and had to begin again,
Poor old Michael Finnegan (begin again) . . . .

There Was an Old Woman Tossed Up in a Basket

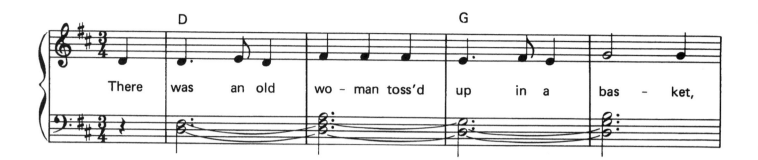

There was an old wo - man toss'd up in a bas - ket,

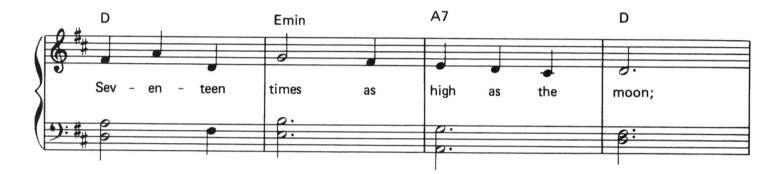

Sev - en - teen times as high as the moon;

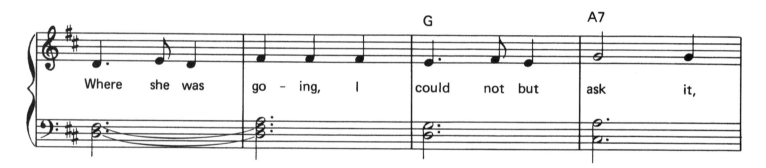

Where she was go - ing, I could not but ask it,

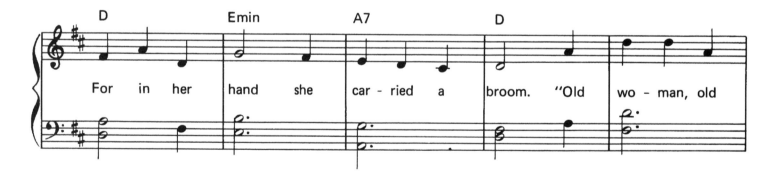

For in her hand she car - ried a broom. "Old wo - man, old

wo - man, old wo - man," quoth I; "O whith - er, O whith - er, O

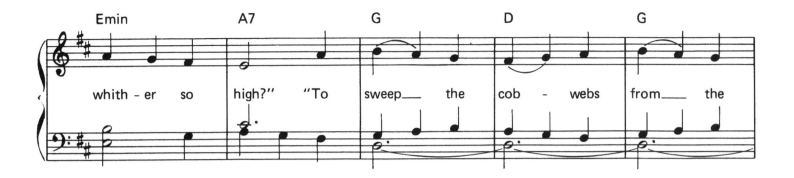

whith - er so high?" "To sweep___ the cob - webs from___ the

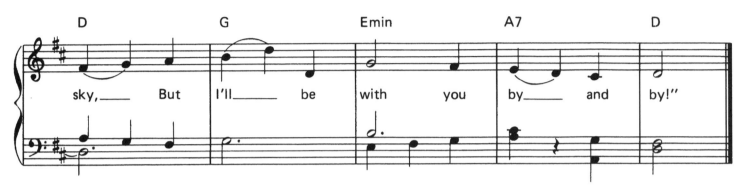

sky,___ But I'll___ be with you by___ and by!"

Hickory Dickory Dock

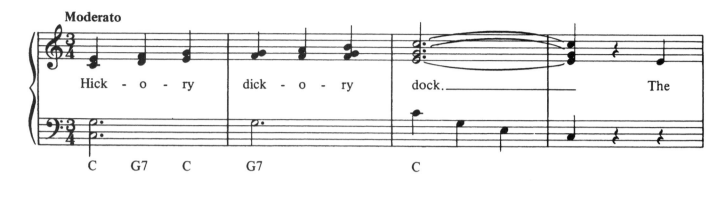

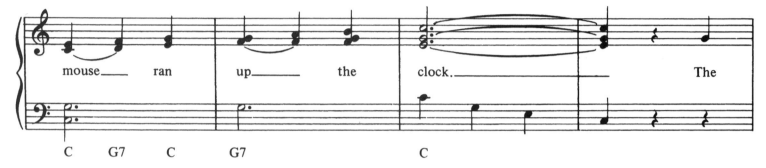

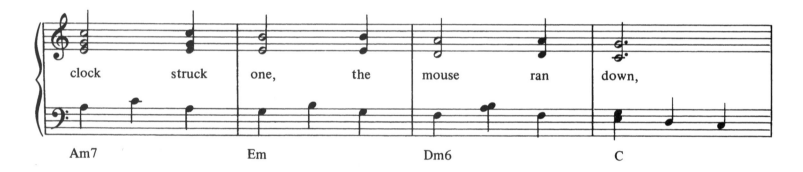

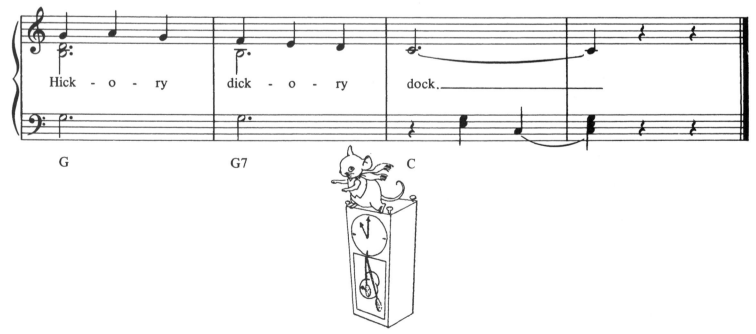

Diddle, Diddle Dumpling

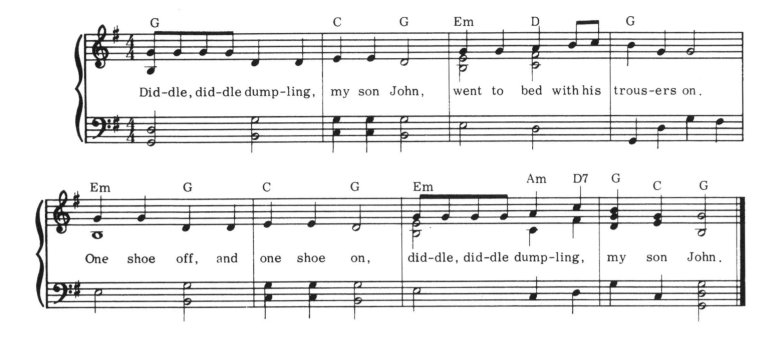

Did-dle, did-dle dump-ling, my son John, went to bed with his trous-ers on.

One shoe off, and one shoe on, did-dle, did-dle dump-ling, my son John.

Dear Old Daddy Whiskers

We have a dear old Dad - dy, whose hair is sil - ver

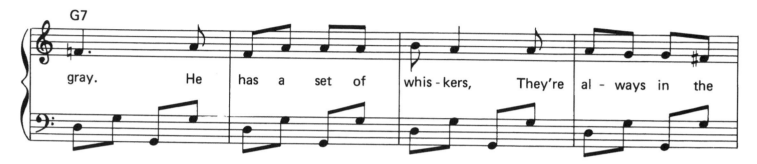

gray. He has a set of whis - kers, They're al - ways in the

Chorus

way. Oh, they're al - ways in the way, The cow eats them for

hay. Moth - er eats them in her sleep, She thinks she's eat - ing

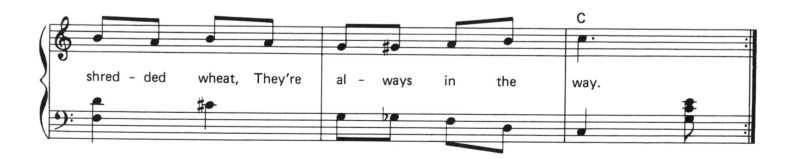

shred - ded wheat, They're al - ways in the way.

We have a dear old Mommy,
She likes his whiskers, too.
She uses them for cleaning
And stirring up a stew.
Chorus:

We have a dear old brother,
Who has a Ford machine.
He uses Daddy's whiskers
To strain the gasoline.
Chorus:

We have a dear old sister.
Her name is Ida Mae.
She climbs up Daddy's whiskers
And braids them every day.
Chorus:

Around the supper table,
We make a merry group,
Until dear Daddy's whiskers
Get tangled in the soup.
Chorus:

Daddy was in battle,
He wasn't killed, you see:
His whiskers looked like bushes,
And fooled the enemy.
Chorus:

When Daddy goes in swimming,
No bathing suit for him.
He ties his whiskers round his waist,
And happily jumps in.
Chorus:

Rub-a-Dub-Dub

Rub-A-Dub-Dub, Three men in a tub, And who d'you think they be?___ The butch-er, the bak-er, the can-dle-stick mak-er, So turn out the knaves, all three.

Pease Porridge Hot

Pease Por-ridge Hot, pease por-ridge cold, pease por-ridge in the pot nine days old!

Mother May I Go Out to Swim?

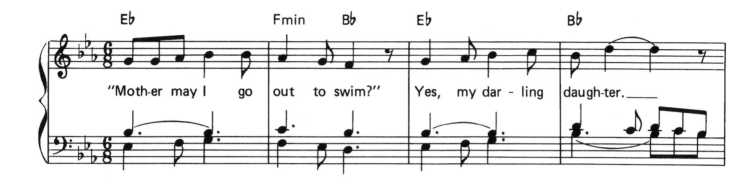

"Moth-er may I go out to swim?" Yes, my dar - ling daugh-ter.____

Hang your clothes on a hick-o-ry limb, But don't go near the wa-ter.____

There's a Hole in the Bucket

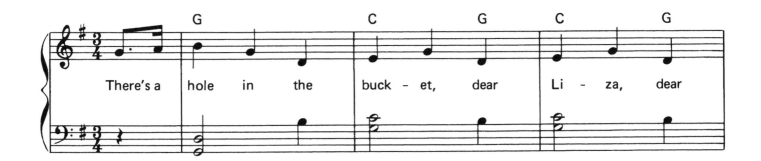

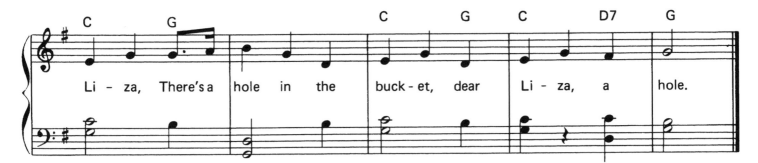

There's a hole in the bucket, dear Liza, dear Liza,
There's a hole in the bucket, dear Liza, a hole.

Then mend it, dear Henry, dear Henry,
Then mend it, dear Henry, dear Henry, mend it.

With what shall I mend it, dear Liza, dear Liza,
With what shall I mend it, dear Liza, with what.

With straw, dear Henry, dear Henry,
With straw, dear Henry, dear Henry, with straw.

The straw is too long, dear Liza, dear Liza,
The straw is too long, dear Liza, dear Liza, too long.

Then cut it, dear Henry, dear Henry,
Then cut it, dear Henry, dear Henry, cut it.

With what shall I cut it, dear Liza, dear Liza,
With what shall I cut it, dear Liza, with what?

With a knife, dear Henry, dear Henry, dear Henry,
With a knife, dear Henry, dear Henry, a knife.

The knife is too dull, dear Liza, dear Liza,
The knife is too dull, dear Liza, too dull.

Then sharpen it, dear Henry, dear Henry, dear Henry,
Then sharpen it, dear Henry, dear Henry, sharpen it.

With what shall I sharpen it, dear Liza, dear Liza,
With what shall I sharpen it, dear Liza, with what?

With a stone, dear Henry, dear Henry, dear Henry,
With a stone, dear Henry, dear Henry, a stone.

The stone is too dry, dear Liza, dear Liza,
The stone is too dry, dear Liza, too dry.

Then wet it, dear Henry, dear Henry, dear Henry,
Then wet it, dear Henry, dear Henry, wet it.

With what shall I wet it, dear Liza, dear Liza,
With what shall I wet it, dear Liza, with what?

With water, dear Henry, dear Henry, dear Henry,
With water, dear Henry, dear Henry, water.

But where shall I get it, dear Liza, dear Liza,
But where shall I get it, dear Liza, but where?

From the well, dear Henry, dear Henry, dear Henry,
From the well, dear Henry, dear Henry, the well.

In what shall I carry it, dear Liza, dear Liza,
In what shall I carry it, dear Liza, in what?

In the bucket, dear Henry, dear Henry, dear Henry,
In the bucket, dear Henry, dear Henry, the bucket.

But there's a hole in the bucket, dear Liza, dear Liza,
There's a hole in the bucket, dear Liza, a hole!

SONGS FOR QUIET TIME

Down in the Valley

Down in the val - ley, _____ the val - ley so
Hear the wind blow, love, _____ oh, hear the wind

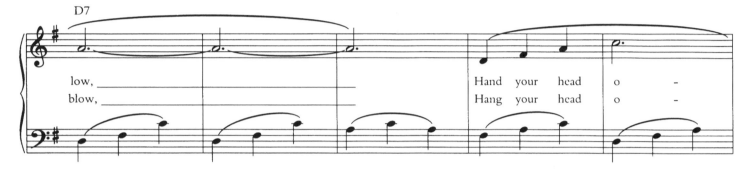

low, _____
blow, _____
Hand your head o -
Hang your head o -

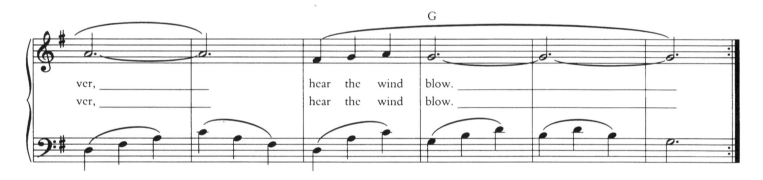

ver, _____ hear the wind blow. _____
ver, _____ hear the wind blow. _____

2. Roses love sunshine, violets love dew,
   Angels in heaven know I love you,
   Know I love you, dear, know I love you,
   Angels in heaven know I love you.

3. If you don't love me, love whom you please,
   Throw your arms 'round me, give my heart ease.
   Give my heart ease, love, give my heart ease,
   Throw your arms 'round me, give my heart ease.

4. Build me a castle forty feet high,
   So I can see him as he rides by.
   As he rides by, love, as he rides by,
   So I can see him as he rides by.

Moonlight Bay

Michael, Row the Boat Ashore

2. Jordan's river is chilly and cold, hallelujah,
   Kills the body, but not the soul, hallelujah.
   Jordan's river is deep and wide, hallelujah,
   Meet my mother on the other side, hallelujah.

3. Michael's boat is a music boat, hallelujah,
   Michael's boat is a music boat, hallelujah,
   Michael, row the boat ashore, hallelujah,
   Michael, row the boat ashore, hallelujah.

Scarborough Fair

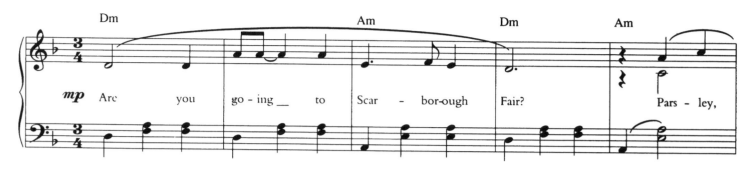

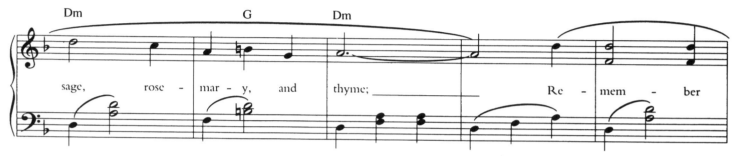

2. Tell her to make me a cambric shirt,
   Parsley, sage, rosemary, and thyme;
   Without a seam or fine needlework,
   And then she'll be true love of mine.

3. Tell her to wash it in yonder dry well,
   Parsley, sage, rosemary, and thyme;
   Where water ne'er sprung, nor drop of rain fell,
   And then she'll be a true love of mine.

4. Tell her to dry it on yonder thorn,
   Parsley, sage, rosemary, and thyme;
   Which never bore blossom since Adam was born,
   And then she'll be a true love of mine.

5. Oh, will you find me an acre of land,
   Parsley, sage, rosemary, and thyme;
   Between the sea foam and the sea sand,
   Or never be a true love of mine?

6. Oh, will you plough it with a lamb's horn,
   Parsley, sage, rosemary, and thyme;
   And sow it all with one peppercorn,
   Or never be a true love of mine?

7. Oh, will you reap it with a sickle of leather,
   Parsley, sage, rosemary, and thyme;
   And tie it up with a peacock's feather,
   Or never be a true love of mine?

8. And when you've done and finished your work,
   Parsley, sage, rosemary, and thyme;
   Then come to me for your cambric shirt,
   And you shall be a true love of mine.

The Riddle Song

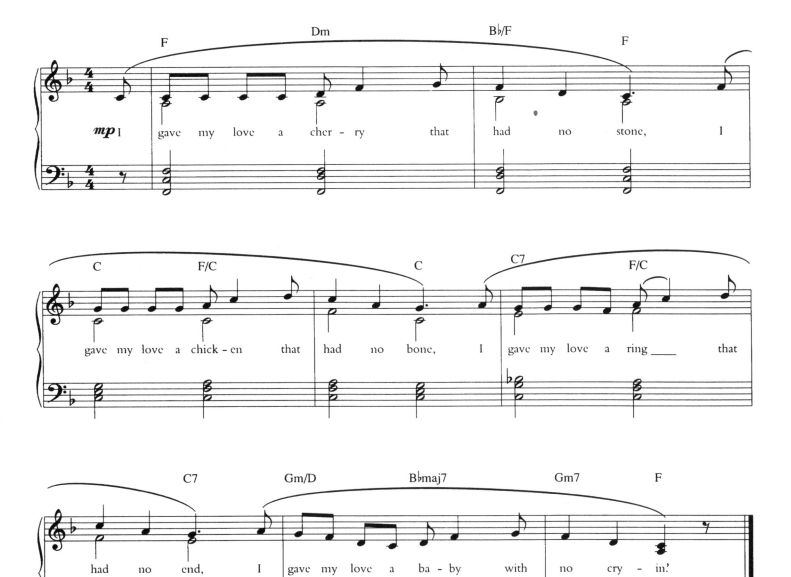

I gave my love a cher-ry that had no stone, I gave my love a chick-en that had no bone, I gave my love a ring____ that had no end, I gave my love a ba-by with no cry-in.'

2. How can there be a cherry that has no stone?
   How can there be a chicken that has no bone?
   How can there be a ring that has no end?
   How can there be a baby with no cryin'?

3. A cherry when it's bloomin' it has no stone,
   A chicken when it's pippin', it has no bone,
   A ring when it's rollin', it has no end,
   A baby when it's sleepin' has no cryin'.

Home on the Range

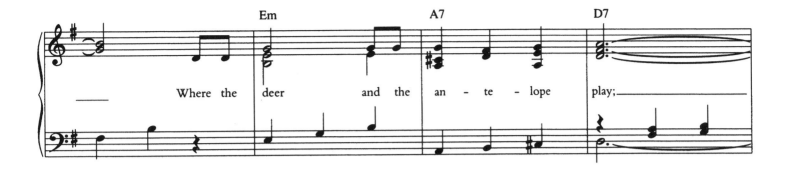

Where the deer and the an-te-lope play;

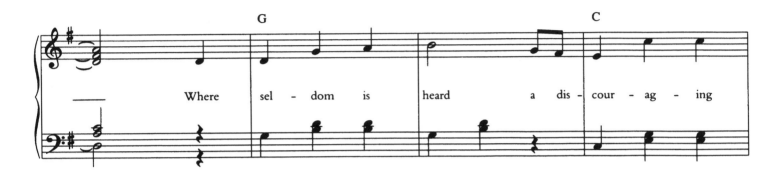

Where sel-dom is heard a dis-cour-ag-ing

word, And the skies are not cloud-y all day.

2. Oh, give me a land where the bright diamond sand,
   Flows leisurely down the stream;
   Where the graceful, white swan goes gliding along,
   Like a maid in a heavenly dream.
   Chorus

3. Where the air is so pure and the zephyrs so free,
   The breezes so balmy and bright;
   That I would not exchange my home on the range,
   For all of the cities so bright.
   Chorus

4. How often at night when the heavens are bright,
   With the light of the glittering stars,
   Have I stood there amazed and asked as I gazed,
   If their glory exceeds that of ours.
   Chorus

Home, Sweet Home

'Mid pleas - ures and pal - a - ces though we may roam,___ Be it
An ex - ile from home splen-dor daz - zles in vain,___ Oh,

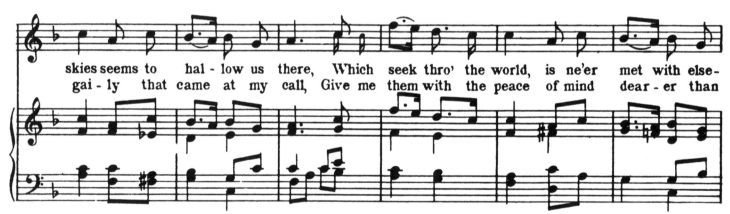

ev - er so hum - ble there's no___ place like home.___ A charm from the
give___ me my low - ly thatched cot - tage a - gain!___ The birds sing-ing

skies seems to hal - low us there, Which seek thro' the world, is ne'er met with else-
gai - ly that came at my call, Give me them with the peace of mind dear - er than

where
all Home! Home! sweet sweet home There's no place like home there's no place like home

Music Everywhere

Mu - sic in the val - ley, Mu - sic on the hill, Mu - sic in the
Mu - sic in the fire - side, Mu - sic in the hall, Mu - sic in the

wood - land, Mu - sic in the rill; Mu - sic on the moun - tain,
school - room, Mu - sic for us all; Mu - sic in our sor - row,

Mu - sic in the air, Mu - sic in the true heart, Mu - sic ev - 'ry - where.
Mu - sic in our care, Mu - sic in our glad - ness, Mu - sic ev - 'ry - where.

Lavender's Blue

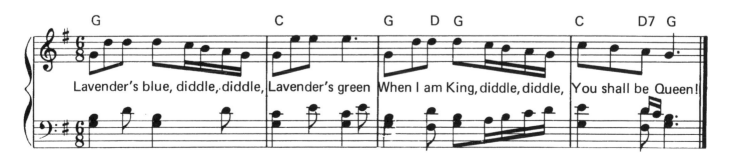

Lavender's blue, diddle, diddle, Lavender's green When I am King, diddle, diddle, You shall be Queen!

Moon and Sun

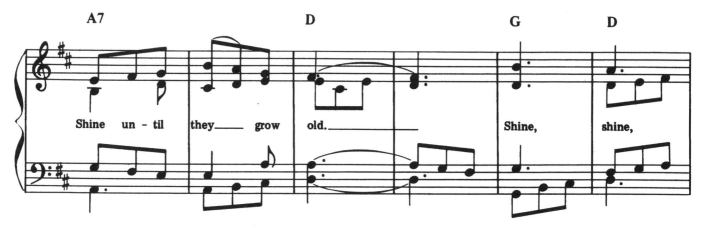

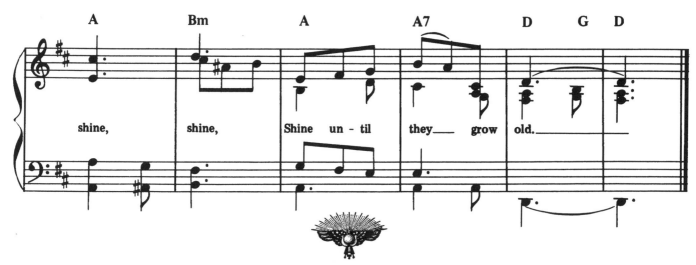

Where Are You Going to, My Pretty Maid?

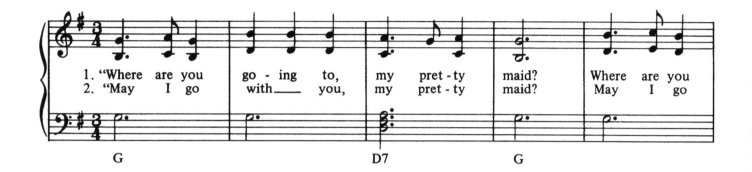

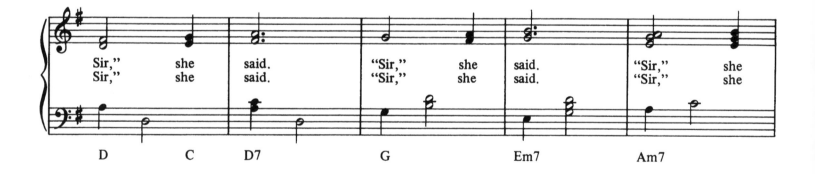

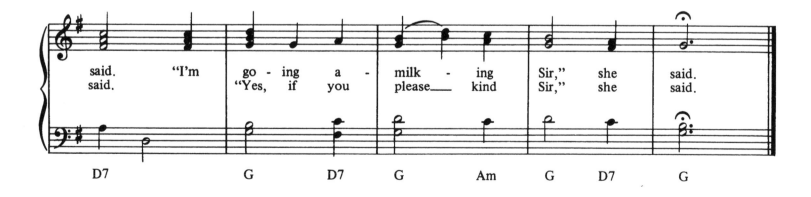

Grandfather's Clock

old man died.

Chorus

Nine-ty years with-out slum-ber-ing,

tick, tock, tick, tock, His life sec-onds num-ber-ing,

tick, tock, tick, tock; It stopped short

nev-er to go a-gain, When the old man died.

2. In watching its pendulum swing to and fro,
   Many hours had he spent while a boy;
   And in childhood and manhood, the clock seemed to know,
   And to share both his grief and his joy;
   For it struck twenty-four when he entered at the door,
   With a blooming and beautiful bride;
   But it stopped short, never to go again,
   When the old man died.
   Chorus

3. My grandfather said that of those he could hire,
   Not a servant so faithful he found;
   For it wasted no time, and had but one desire,
   At the close of each week, to be wound;
   And it kept in its place, not a frown upon its face,
   And its hands never hung by its side;
   But it stopped short, never to go again,
   When the old man died.
   Chorus

4. It rang an alarm in the dead of the night,
   An alarm that, for years, had been dumb;
   And we knew that his spirit was pluming its flight,
   That his hour of departure had come.
   Still the clock kept the time, with a soft and muffled chime,
   As we silently stood by his side;
   But it stopped short, never to go again,
   When the old man died.
   Chorus

Shenandoah

2. Oh, Shenandoah, I love your daughter,
   Away, you rolling river,
   For her I'd cross your roaming water,
   Away, I'm bound away,
   'Cross the wide Missouri.

3. Oh, Shenandoah, I'm bound to leave you,
   Away, you rolling river,
   Oh, Shenandoah, I'll not deceive you,
   Away, I'm bound away,
   'Cross the wide Missouri.

Song Adventures and Make-Believe Lands

The Man in the Moon

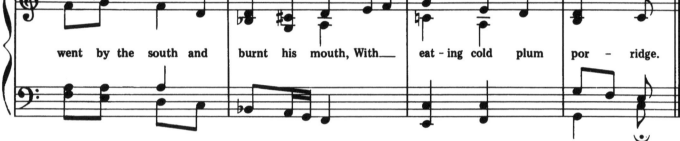

The man in the moon came down too soon, And asked his way to Nor - wich, He

went by the south and burnt his mouth, With__ eat - ing cold plum por - ridge.

Take Me Out to the Ball Game

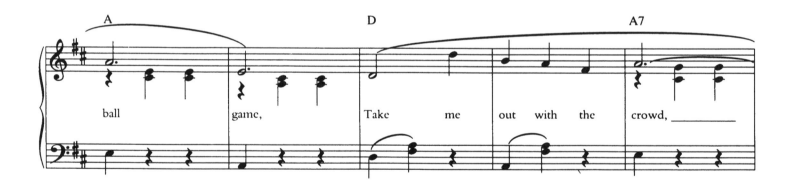

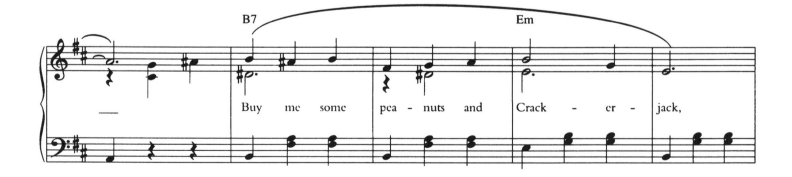

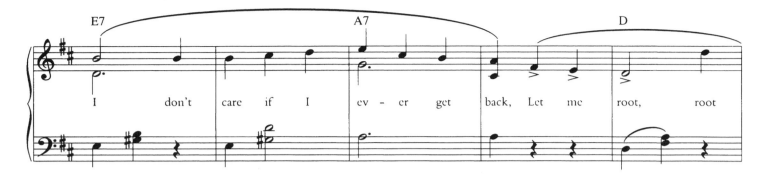

I don't care if I ev-er get back, Let me root, root

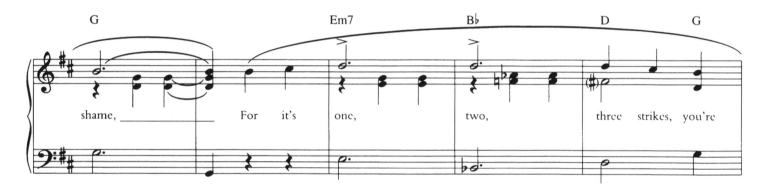

root for the home team, If they don't win it's a

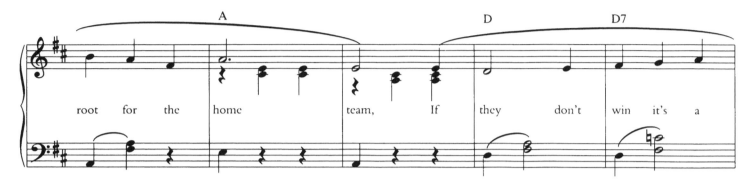

shame, _____ For it's one, two, three strikes, you're

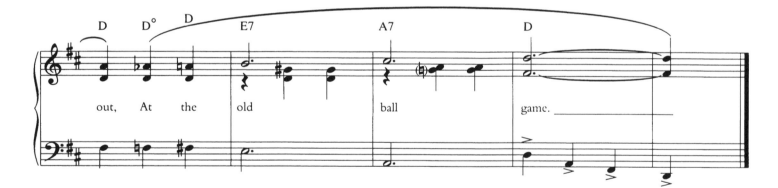

out, At the old ball game. _____

Hey Diddle Diddle

Hey did - dle did - dle, the cat and the fid - dle, the

F — C7 Bb C7 — F — C7 Bb C7

cow jumped ov - er the moon. The

F — D7 — Gm — C Cdim

lit - tle dog laughed to see such fun and the

Gm7 — Eb — Bb — Gm C Gm7

dish ran a - way with the spoon.

F Bb F C7 F Gm7 F

The Lost Doll

1. I once had a sweet lit-tle doll, dears, The pret-ti-est doll in the world; Her
2. I found my poor lit-tle doll, dears, As I played in the heath one day; Folks

cheeks were so red and so white, dears, And her hair was so charm-ing-ly curled, But I
say she is ter-ri-bly changed, dears, For her paint is all washed a-way, And her

lost my poor lit-tle doll, dears, As I played in the heath one day, And I
arm trod-den off by the cows, dears, And her hair not the least bit curled, Yet for

cried for more than a week, dears, But I nev-er could find where she lay.
old sake's sake, she is still, dears, The pret-ti-est doll in the world.

The Erie Canal

I've got a mule, ___ her name is Sal,

Fif - teen miles ___ on the E - rie Ca - nal. ___ She's a

good old work - er and a good old pal, Fif - teen miles ___ on the

E - rie Ca - nal. ___ We've hauled some barg - es in our day,

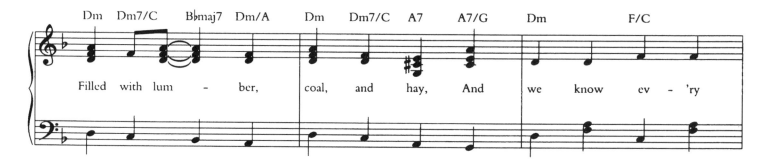

Filled with lum - ber, coal, and hay, And we know ev - 'ry

inch of the way, From Al-ban-y _____ to _____ Buf-fa-lo. _____

Chorus

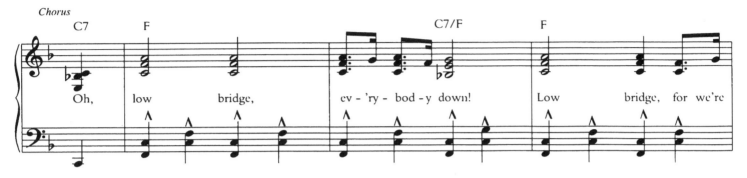

Oh, low bridge, ev-'ry-bod-y down! Low bridge, for we're

com-ing to a town! And you'll al-ways know your neigh-bor, you'll

al-ways know your pal, If you've ev-er nav-i-gat-ed on the E-rie Can-al.

2. We'd better look around for a job, old gal,
Fifteen miles on the Erie Canal.
'Cause you bet your life I'd never part with Sal,
Fifteen miles on the Erie Canal.
Get up there, mule, here comes a lock,
We'll make Rome 'bout six o'clock,
One more trip and back we'll go,
Right back home to Buffalo.
Chorus

I Saw a Ship A-Sailing

King Arthur

When good King Ar-thur ruled this land, He was a wise old king, He

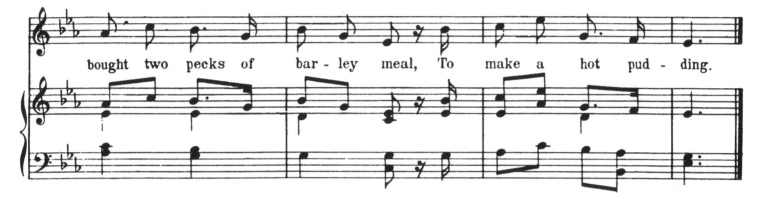

bought two pecks of bar-ley meal, To make a hot pud-ding.

Will You Walk a Little Faster?

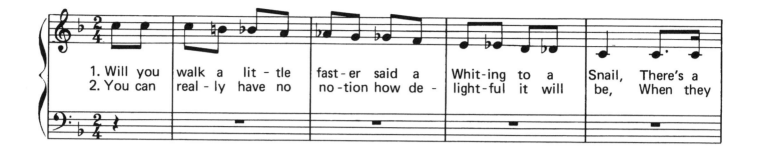

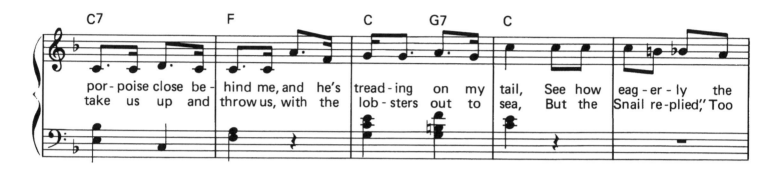

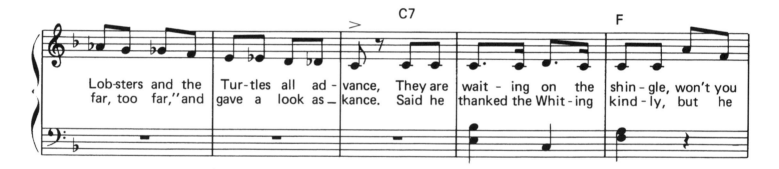

If All the World Were Paper

If all the world were pa - per, And all the sea were ink____ And

all the trees were bread and cheese, What should we do for drink?____

Oh, Susanna

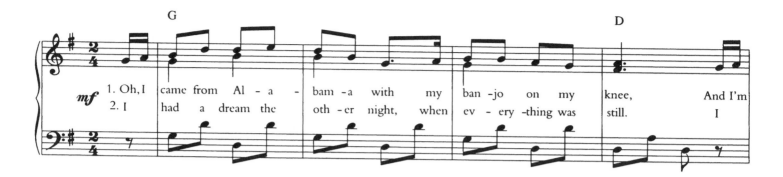

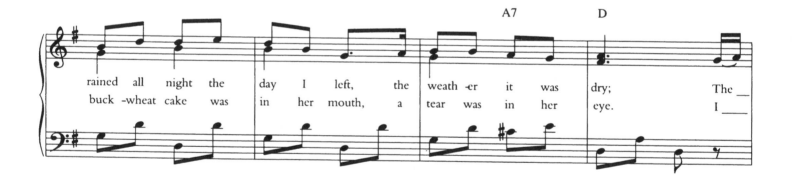

Chorus

Oh, Su - san - na, Oh, don't you cry for me. I

come from Al - a - bam - a with my ban - jo on my knee.

Sailing, Sailing

Sail - ing, Sail - ing, o - ver the bound - ing main, _____ For

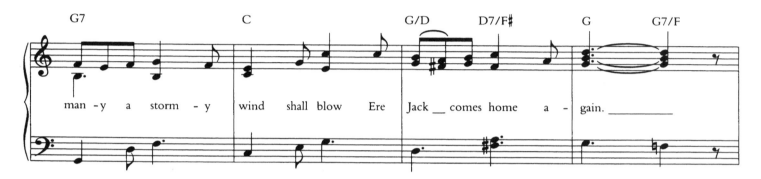

man - y a storm - y wind shall blow Ere Jack __ comes home a - gain. _____

Sail - ing, sail - ing, o - ver the bound - ing main, _____ For

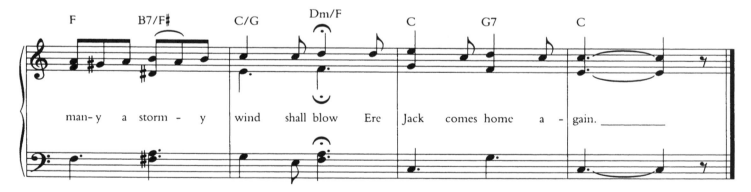

man - y a storm - y wind shall blow Ere Jack comes home a - gain. _____

The Teddy Bears' Picnic

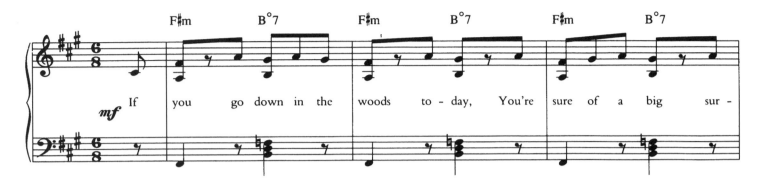

If you go down in the woods to-day, You're sure of a big sur-

prise. _____ If you go down in the woods to-day, You'd bet-ter go in dis-

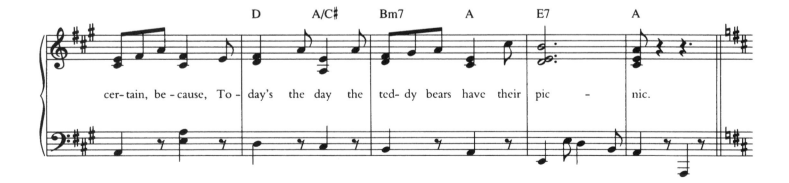

guise; _____ For ev-'ry bear that ev-er there was Will gath-er there for

cer-tain, be-cause, To-day's the day the ted-dy bears have their pic - nic.

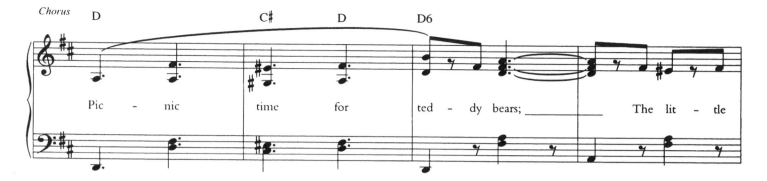

Pic - nic time for ted - dy bears; _____ The lit - tle

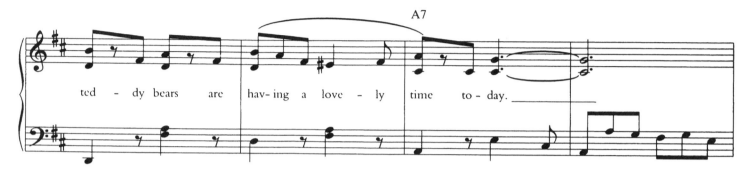

ted - dy bears are hav-ing a love - ly time to-day. _____

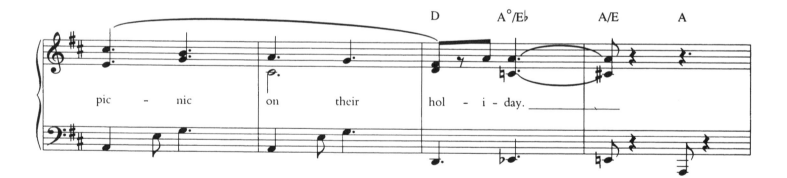

Watch them, catch them un - a-wares, _____ And see them

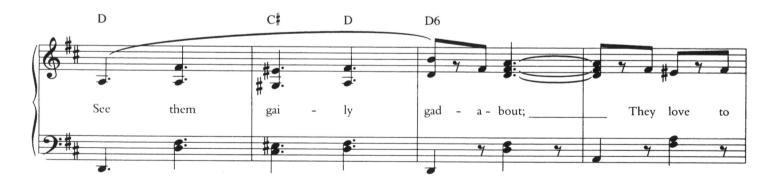

pic - nic on their hol - i-day. _____

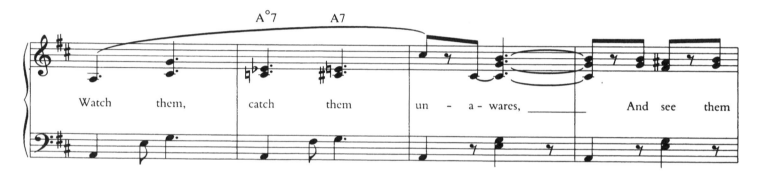

See them gai - ly gad - a-bout; _____ They love to

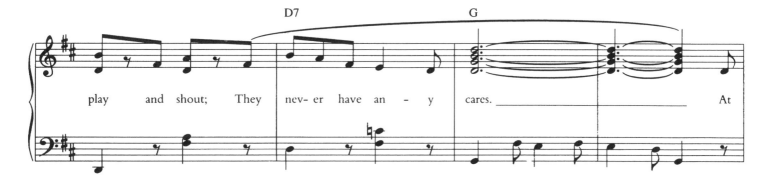

play and shout; They nev- er have an — y cares. _____ At

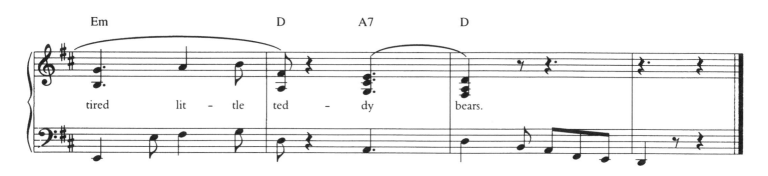

six o' - clock their mum — mies and dad — dies will take them home to bed, Be — cause they're

tired lit — tle ted — dy bears.

2. Ev'ry teddy bear who's been good
   Is sure of a treat today.
   There's lots of marvelous things to eat,
   And wonderful games to play.
   Beneath the trees where nobody sees,
   They'll hide and seek as long as they please,
   'Cause that's the way the teddy bears have their picnic.
   Chorus

3. If you go down in the woods today,
   You'd better not go alone.
   It's lovely down in the woods today,
   But safer to stay at home.
   For ev'ry bear that ever there was
   Will gather there for certain, because
   Today's the day the teddy bears have their picnic.
   Chorus

Toyland

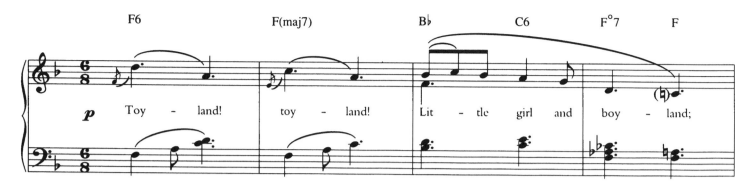

Toy - land! toy - land! Lit - tle girl and boy - land;

While you dwell with - in it, _____ You are ev - er hap - py then.

Child - hood's joy - land, Mys - tic, mer - ry toy - land;

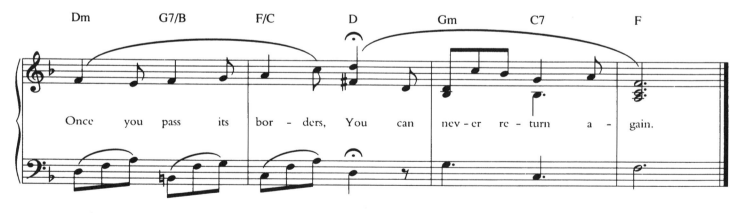

Once you pass its bor - ders, You can nev - er re - turn a - gain.

SLEEPYTIME

Rock-a-Bye Baby

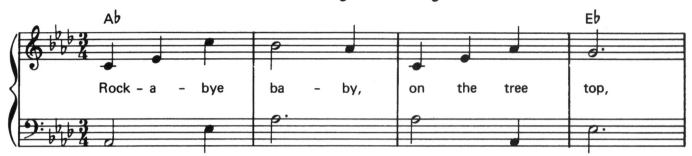

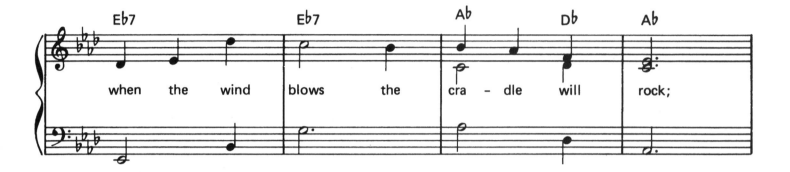

Rock - a - bye   ba - by,   on   the   tree   top,

when   the   wind   blows   the   cra - dle   will   rock;

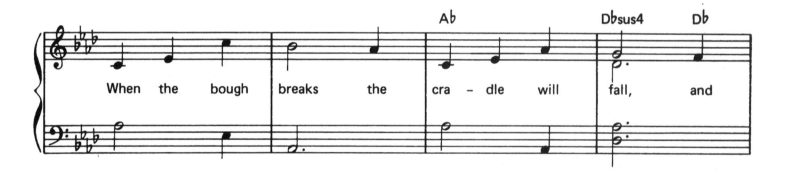

When   the   bough   breaks   the   cra - dle   will   fall,   and

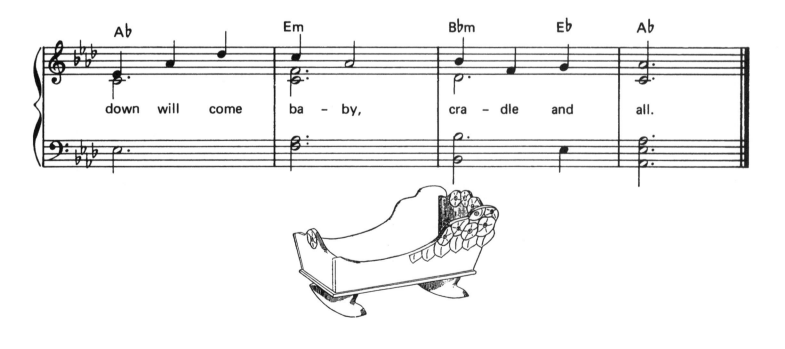

down   will   come   ba - by,   cra - dle   and   all.

Golden Slumbers

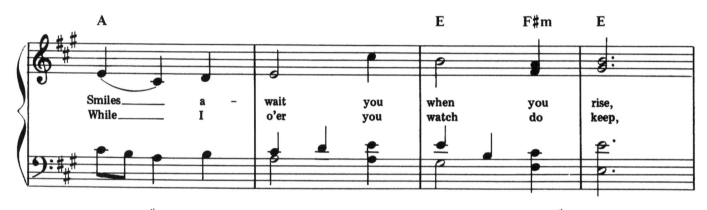

All the Pretty Little Horses

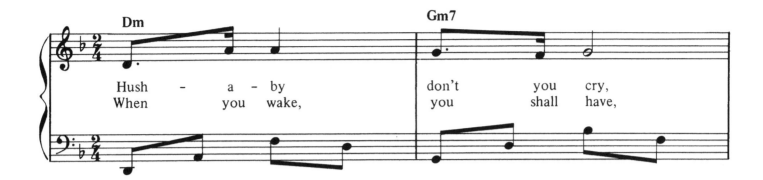

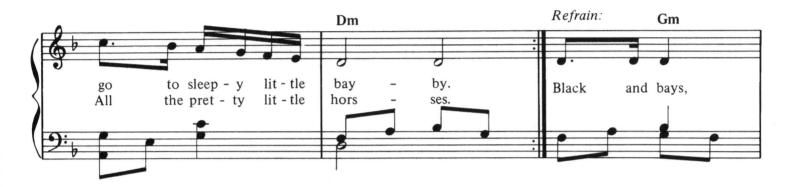

Hush — a - by   don't   you   cry,
When   you wake,   you   shall   have,

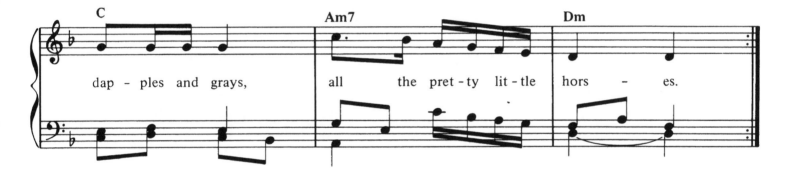

go   to sleep - y   lit - tle   bay — by.   *Refrain:*   Black   and bays,
All   the pret - ty   lit - tle   hors — ses.

dap - ples and grays,   all   the pret - ty lit - tle   hors — es.

Sweet and Low

Sleep and Rest

1. Sleep, oh, my dar - ling, and rest,
   Birds are a - sleep in their nest,

2. Lis - ten, no sound can be heard,
   Through the house noth-ing has stirred,

Gar - den and mead - ow are still,
Bees hum no more by the rill,

Lit - tle gray mouse is not near,
Cel - lar and kitch-en are clear,

In through the win - dow so bright
Shines the moon's sil - ver - y light;

On - ly my ba - by so bright
Ly - ing a - wake in the night;

Nes - tle your head on my breast;
Sleep, oh, my dar - ling, and rest;
oh, sleep, and rest.

Dance to Your Daddy

Dance to your dad - dy, My lit - tle lad - die,

Dance to your dad - dy, My lit - tle man.

Verse:

You shall have a fish - y In your lit - tle dish - y,

You shall have a fish - y When the boat comes in.

Extra Verses

You shall have a coaty, and a pair of britches,
You shall have a coaty, when the ship comes in.
(Chorus)

When you are a man and come to take a wife,
You shall wed a lass and love her all your life.
(Chorus)

Bedtime

1. The eve - ning is com - ing, The sun sinks to rest, The
2. The flow - ers are clos - ing, The dai - sy's a - sleep, The

crows are all fly - ing straight home to the nest. "Caw" says the crow as he
prim - rose is bur - ied in slum - ber so deep, Closed for the night are the

flies o - ver - head, "It's time lit - tle peo - ple were go - ing to bed!"
ros - es so red, "It's time lit - tle peo - ple were go - ing to bed!"

Winkum, Winkum

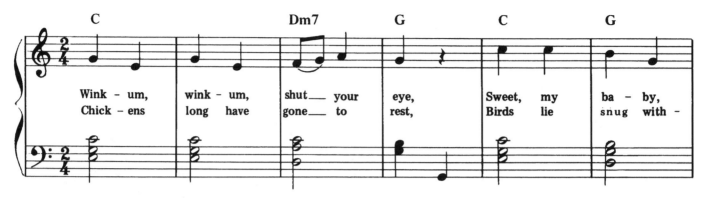

Wink - um, winkum, shut __ your eye,   Sweet, my ba - by,
Chick - ens long have gone __ to rest,   Birds lie snug with -

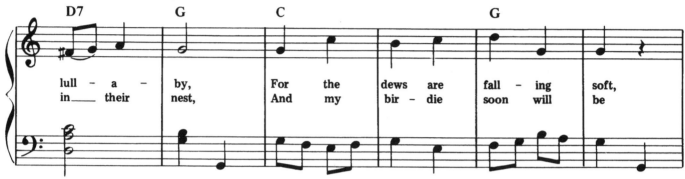

lull - a - by,   For the dews are fall - ing soft,
in __ their nest,   And my bir - die soon will be

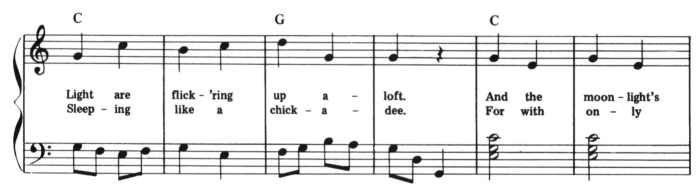

Light are flick - 'ring up a - loft.   And the moon - light's
Sleep - ing like a chick - a - dee.   For with on - ly

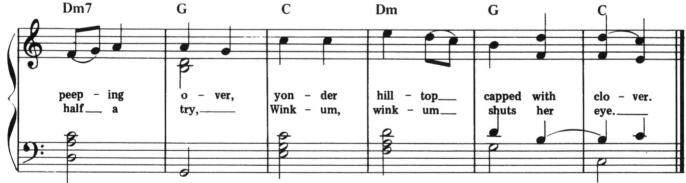

peep - ing o - ver,   yon - der hill - top __ capped with clo - ver.
half __ a try, __   Wink - um, wink - um __ shuts her eye. __

Day and Night

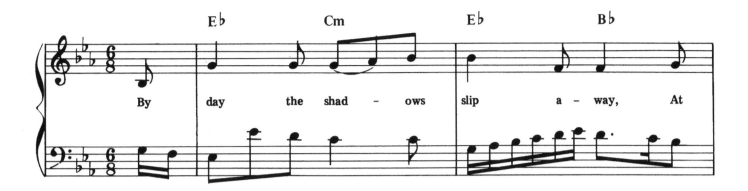

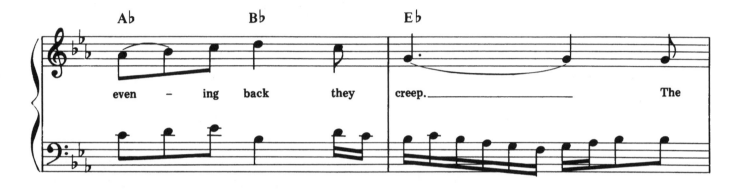

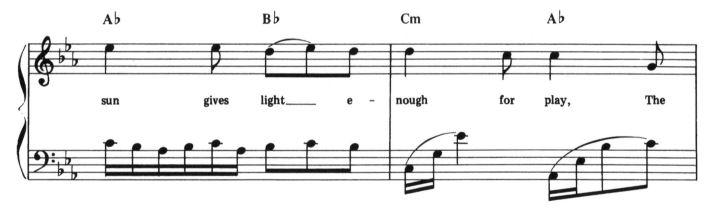

Twinkle, Twinkle Little Star

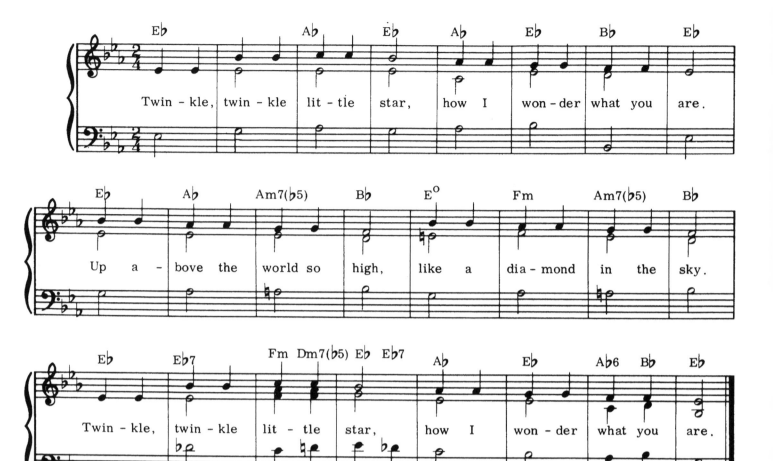

All the World Is Sleeping

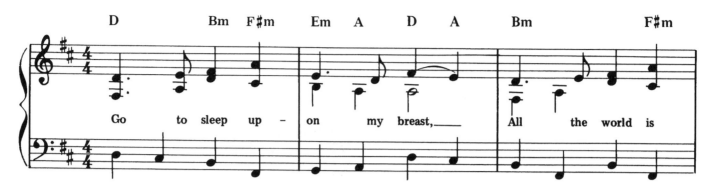

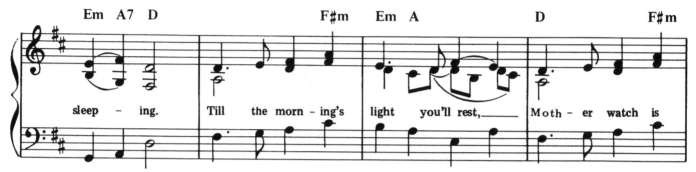

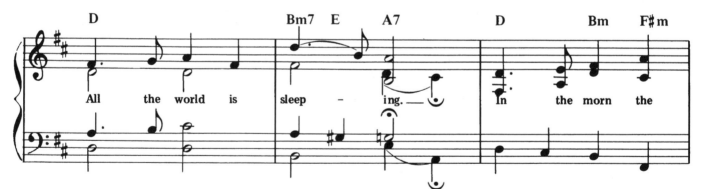

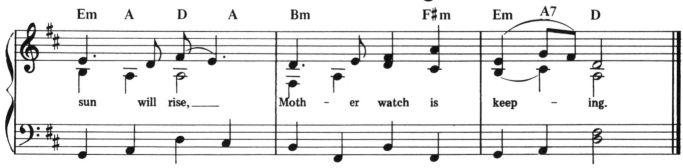

158

Now the Day Is Over

Now the day is o - ver, Night is draw - ing nigh,

Shad - ows of the even - ing Steal a - cross the sky.

Rock the Cradle

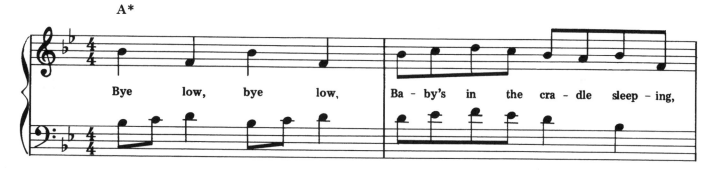

Bye low, bye low, Ba - by's in the cra - dle sleep - ing,

Tip toe, tip toe, still as pus - sy sly - ly creep - ing, Bye low, bye low,

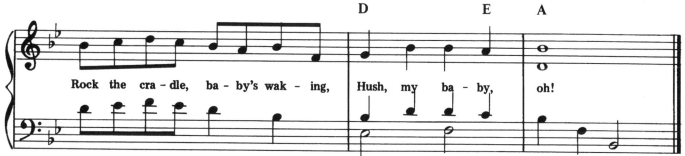

Rock the cra - dle, ba - by's wak - ing, Hush, my ba - by, oh!

*These chords are for guitar with capo on the first fret.

All through the Night

Hush, Little Baby

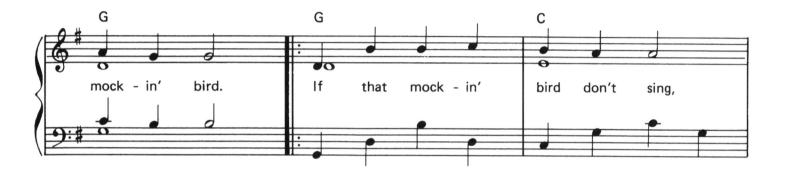

Hush little baby don't say a word,
Mama's gonna buy you a mockin' - bird.

If that mockin' - bird don't sing,
Papa's gonna buy you a diamond ring.

If that ring is made of brass,
Mama's gonna buy you a lookin' glass.

If that lookin' glass gets broke,
Papa's gonna buy you a billy goat.

If that billy goat don't pull,
Mama's gonna buy you a cart and bull.

If that cart and bull turn over,
Papa's gonna buy you a dog named Rover.

If that dog named Rover don't bark,
Mama's gonna buy you a horse and cart.

It that horse and cart fall down,
You'll be the sweetest little boy in town!

Brahms Lullaby

Lull - a - by,   and good   night,   In the   sky   stars   are

bright___ Round your   head,___   flow - ers   gay,___   scent   your   slum - bers   till

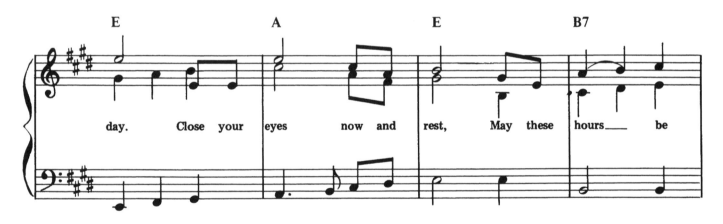

day.   Close your   eyes   now and   rest,   May these   hours___   be

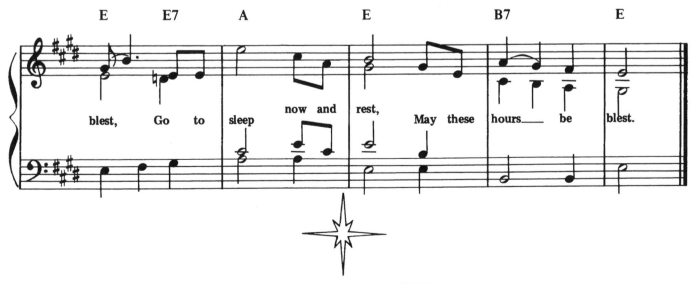

blest,   Go   to   sleep   now and   rest,   May these   hours___   be   blest.

ROUNDS

Come Away

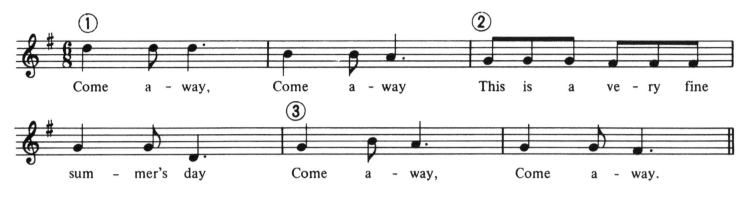

Come a - way, Come a - way This is a ve - ry fine

sum - mer's day Come a - way, Come a - way.

Sweetly Sings the Donkey

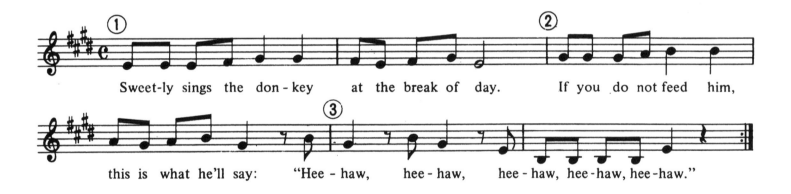

Sweet-ly sings the don-key at the break of day. If you do not feed him,

this is what he'll say: "Hee - haw, hee - haw, hee - haw, hee - haw, hee - haw."

Come, Let's Sing a Merry Round

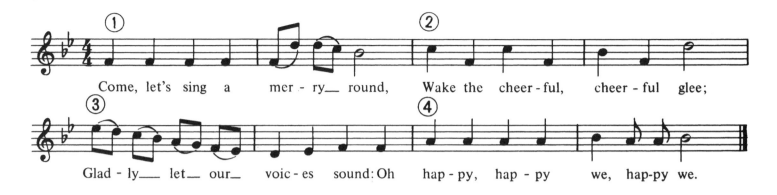

Come, let's sing a mer-ry round, Wake the cheer-ful, cheer-ful glee;
Glad-ly let our voic-es sound: Oh hap-py, hap-py we, hap-py we.

Fruitful Fields Are Waving

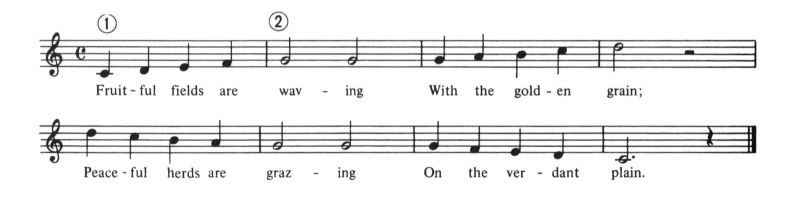

Fruit-ful fields are wav - ing With the gold-en grain;
Peace-ful herds are graz - ing On the ver-dant plain.

O How Lovely Is the Evening

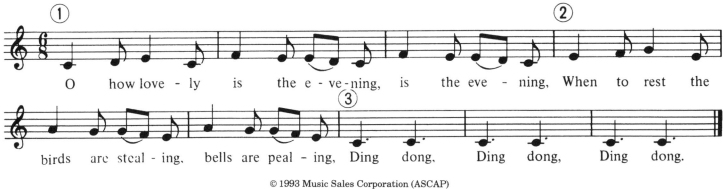

O how love - ly is the e - ve - ning, is the eve - ning, When to rest the birds are steal - ing, bells are peal - ing, Ding dong, Ding dong, Ding dong.

A Lame, Tame Crane

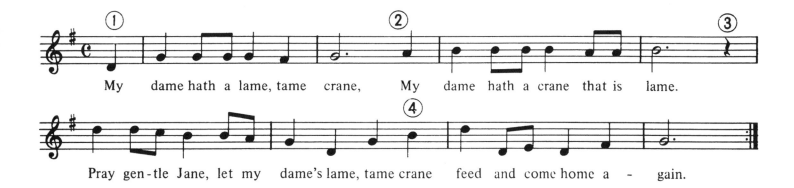

My dame hath a lame, tame crane, My dame hath a crane that is lame.

Pray gen - tle Jane, let my dame's lame, tame crane feed and come home a - gain.

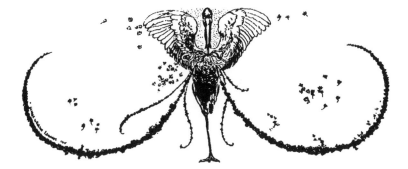

Hey Ho, Nobody's Home

Hey ho, no-bod-y's home, No meat, nor drink, nor mon-ey have I none, Still I will be mer - ry, __ Hey ho, no-bod-y's home, No meat, nor drink, nor mon-ey have I none, Still I will be mer - ry __ Hey ho, no - bod-y's home. __

Merrily, Merrily Greet the Morn

Mer-ri - ly, mer-ri-ly greet the morn, Chee-ri - ly, cheeri - ly sound the horn, Hark! to the ech-oes! Hear them play O'er hill and dale and far a - way.

Dona Nobis Pacem

Do - na   no - bis   pa - cem,   pa - cem,

Do - na__ no - bis   pa   -   cem.   Do -

na   no - bis   pa - cem,   Do - na   no - bis

pa   -   cem.   Do   -   na   no - bis__

pa - cem,   Do - na   no - bis   pa   -   cem.

The Plumtree

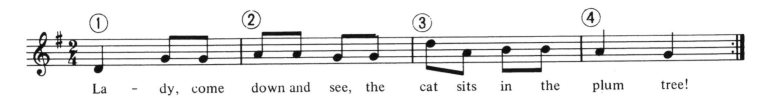

La - dy, come down and see, the cat sits in the plum tree!

Over the Mountain

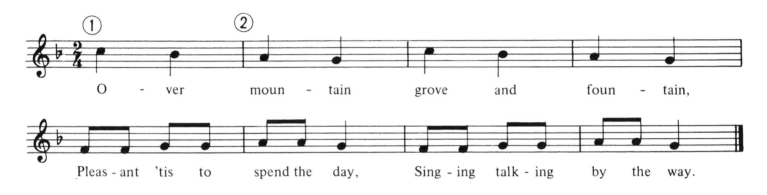

O - ver moun - tain grove and foun - tain,

Pleas - ant 'tis to spend the day, Sing - ing talk - ing by the way.

Who Comes Laughing?

Who comes laugh - ing, laugh - ing, laugh - ing, who comes laugh - ing here a - gain?

We come laugh - ing, Ha ha ha ha ha ha ha ha, we come laugh - ing here a - gain.

Ha ha ha ha ha ha ha ha, ha ha ha ha ha ha ha ha ha, ha ha ha ha ha ha ha ha ha, ha ha ha ha ha!

Now We'll Make the Rafters Ring

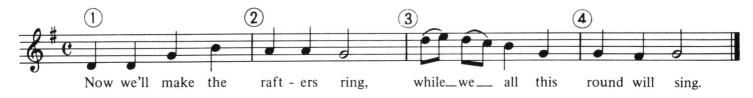

Now we'll make the raf-ers ring, while we all this round will sing.

Thirty Days Hath September

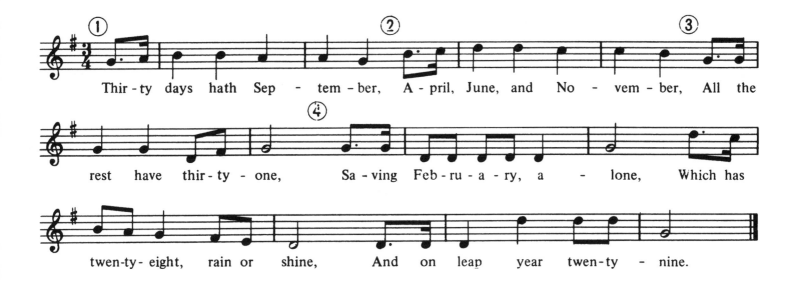

Thir-ty days hath Sep-tem-ber, A-pril, June, and No-vem-ber, All the rest have thir-ty-one, Sa-ving Feb-ru-a-ry, a-lone, Which has twen-ty-eight, rain or shine, And on leap year twen-ty-nine.

Row, Row, Row Your Boat

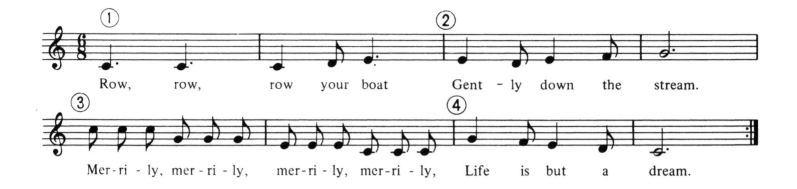

Row, row, row your boat Gent - ly down the stream.

Mer - ri - ly, mer - ri - ly, mer - ri - ly, mer - ri - ly, Life is but a dream.

Love Your Neighbor

Love your neigh - bor live by la - bor would you pros - per that's the way.

Sing Together Merrily

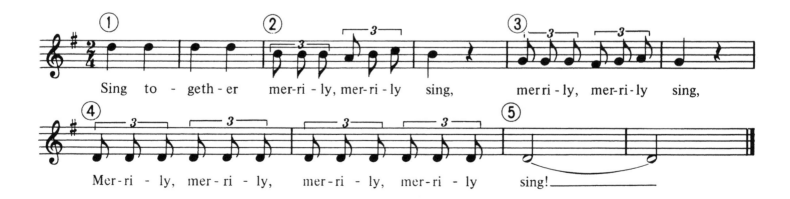

Sing to - geth - er mer - ri - ly, mer - ri - ly sing, mer - ri - ly, mer - ri - ly sing,

Mer - ri - ly, mer - ri - ly, mer - ri - ly, mer - ri - ly sing!

Scotland's Burning

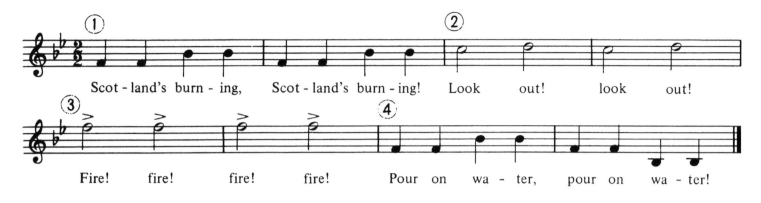

Scot - land's burn - ing, Scot - land's burn - ing! Look out! look out!

Fire! fire! fire! fire! Pour on wa - ter, pour on wa - ter!

My Goose and Thy Goose

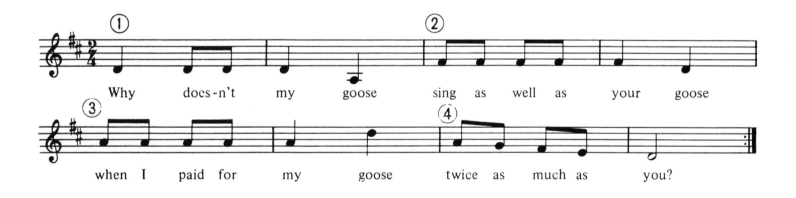

Why does-n't my goose sing as well as your goose

when I paid for my goose twice as much as you?

White Sand, Grey Sand

White sand and grey sand, Who'll buy my white sand? Who'll buy my grey sand?

If I Know What You Know

If I know what you know and you know what I know, then

I know what you know and you know what I know.

Then I know what you know, then I know what

you know and you know, and you know what I know.

Then I know what you know, and you know what I know,

then I know what you know and you know what I know!

Jolly Round

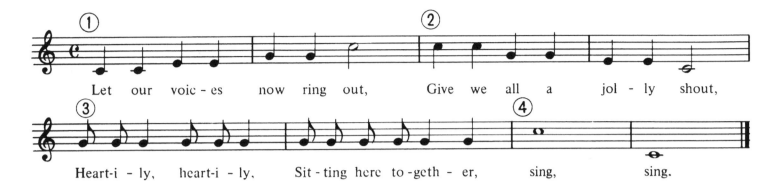

Let our voic-es now ring out, Give we all a jol-ly shout,

Heart-i-ly, heart-i-ly, Sit-ting here to-geth-er, sing, sing.

Onward, Upward

On-ward, up-ward, be our mot-to day by day;

Striv-ing ev-er, learn-ing what of good we may.

White Coral Bells

White co - ral bells u - pon a slen - der stock.

Li - lies of the val - ley deck our gar - den walk. O don't you wish that

you could hear them ring? That can hap - pen on - ly when the fai - ries sing.

Goodbye

Now we say fare - well, Our pleas - ant work is done; Good -

bye then, good - bye then, all, Un - til to - mor - row's sun.

SONGS OF MANY LANDS

Kumbaya

West African folk song

Kum -bay -a, my Lord, Kum -bay -a, Kum -bay -a, my Lord, Kum -bay -a, Kum -bay -a, my Lord, Kum -bay a, Oh, Lord, Kum -bay -a.

2. Someone's crying, Lord, kumbaya, *etc.*

3. Someone's singing, Lord, kumbaya,

4. Someone's praying, Lord, kumbaya,

5. Someone's sleeping, Lord, kumbaya,

Alouette

Canadian folk song

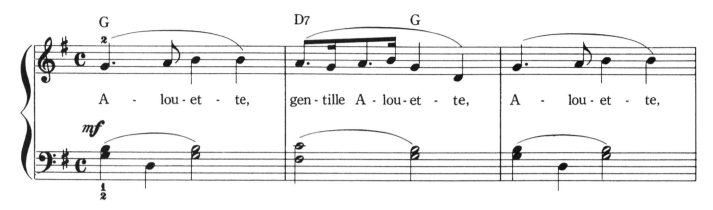

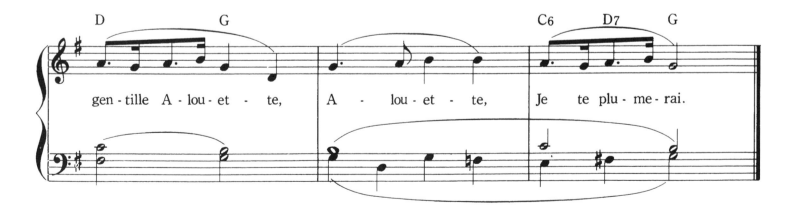

London Bridge

English folk song

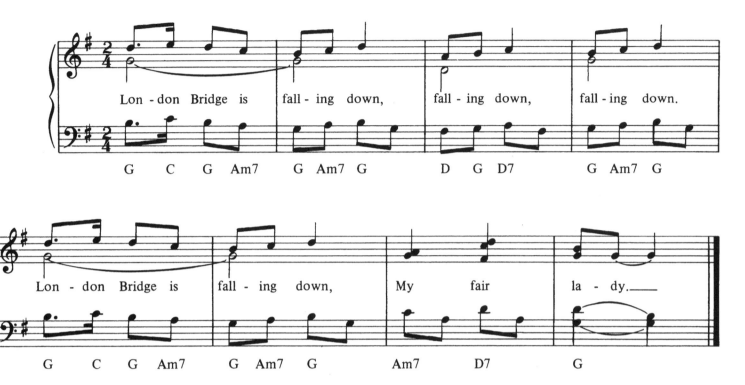

Lon - don Bridge is | fall - ing down, | fall - ing down, | fall - ing down.

G   C   G Am7 | G Am7 G | D   G   D7 | G   Am7   G

Lon - don Bridge is | fall - ing down, | My   fair | la - dy.___

G   C   G Am7 | G Am7 G | Am7   D7 | G

Chiapanecas

Mexican hat dance

Funiculi, Funicula

Italian air

1. Some think___ the world is made for fun and frol-ic, ___And so do I!___
2. Ah, me!___ 'tis strange that some should take to sigh-ing, ___And like it well!___

___And so do I!___ Some think___ it well to be all mel-an-chol-ic, ___To pine and
___And like it well!___ For me,___ I have not thought it worth the try-ing, ___So can-not

sigh;___ To pine and sigh;___ But I___ I love to spend my time in singing,
tell!___ So can-not tell!___ With laugh,___ with dance and song the day soon passes___

___Some joy-ous song,___ Some joy-ous song,___ To set___ the air with music brave-ly
___Full soon is gone,___ Full soon is gone,___ For mirth___ was made for joyous lads and

ring-ing___ Is far from wrong!___ Is far from wrong!___ Lis - ten, lis - ten,
lass-es___ To call their own!___ To call their own!___ Lis - ten, lis - ten,

CHORUS

Ech-oes sound a - far! ___ Lis - ten, lis - ten, Echoes sound a-far! Fu-ni-cu-li, fu-ni-cu-
Hark the soft gui-tar! ___ Lis - ten, lis - ten, Hark the soft gui-tar! Fu-ni-cu-li, fu-ni-cu-

la, fu-ni-cu-li, fu-ni-cu-la! Ech-oes sound a - far, Fu-ni-cu-li, fu-ni-cu-la!
la, fu-ni-cu-li, fu-ni-cu-la! Hark the soft gui-tar! Fu-ni-cu-li, fu-ni-cu-la!

Cockles and Mussels

Irish folk song

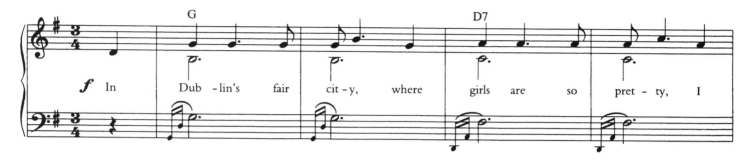

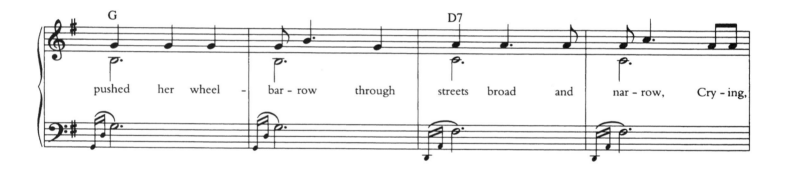

Chorus

A - live, a - live - o! ___ a - live, a - live - o!" ___ Cry - ing,

"Cock - les and mus - sels, a - live, a - live - o!"

2. She was a fishmonger, but sure 'twas no wonder,
   For so were her father and mother before,
   And they pushed their wheelbarrow,
   Through streets broad and narrow,
   Crying, "Cockles and mussels, alive, alive-o!"
   Chorus

Au Clair de la Lune

(In the Moonlight Bright)

French folk song

O' Mein Lieber Augustin

German folk song

O' mein lie-ber Au-gus-tin, Au-gus-tin, Au-gus-tin, O' mein lie-ber Au-gus-tin al-les-ist weg:

Bock ist weg stock ist weg Auch ich bin in dem dreck O' mein lie-ber Au-gus-tin, al-lest is weg.

Song of the Volga Boatman

Russian folk song

Let's be hap - py lads as we pull on Sing this song __ from __

night till dawn Ay - da - da - ay - da - da - ay - da - da - ay - da

Pull my brave __ lads pull __ once more Yo __ heave ho

Yo __ heave ho Hm _____

Tum-Balalayka

Yiddish folk song

Verse:

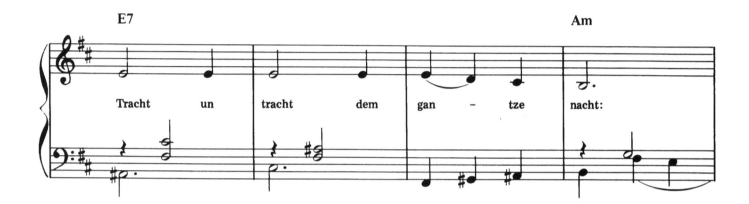

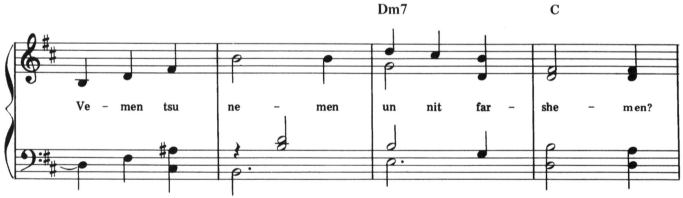

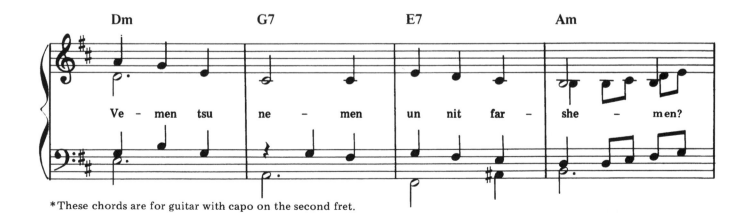

*These chords are for guitar with capo on the second fret.

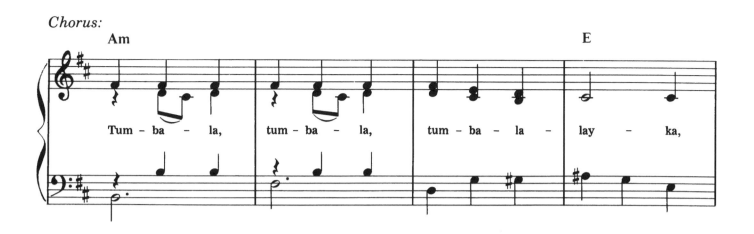

Tum – ba – la, tum – ba – la, tum – ba – la – lay – ka,

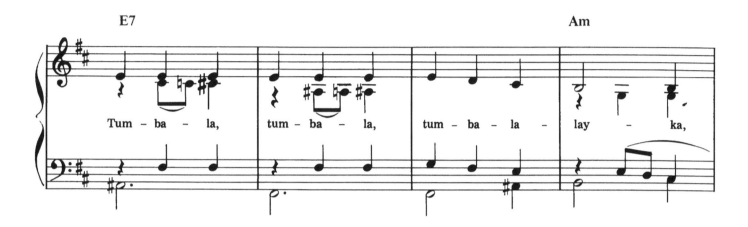

Tum – ba – la, tum – ba – la, tum – ba – la – lay – ka,

Tum – ba – la – lay – ka, shpil ba – la – lay – ka,

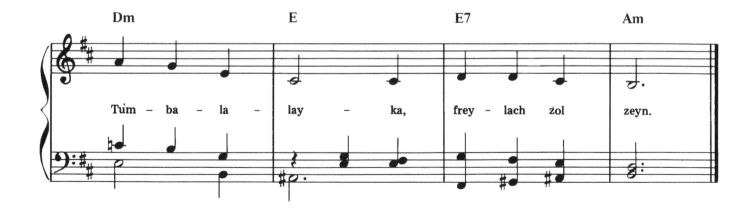

Tum – ba – la – lay – ka, frey – lach żol zeyn.

Extra Verses

2 Meydl, meydl, ch'vel bay dir fregn:
Vos kon vaksn on regn?
Vos kon brenen un nit oyfhern?
Vos kon benken, veynen on trern?

3 Narisher bocher, vos darfstu fregn?
A shteyn kon vaksn, vaksn on regn.
Libe kon brenen, un nit oyfhern.
A harts kon benken, veynen on trern?

English Lyrics

1 A lad stood thinking all the night through,
Thinking, thinking, what to do?
Whose heart to take? Whose heart not to break?
Whose heart to take? Whose heart not to break?

*Tum-bala, tum-bala, tum-balalayka
Tum-bala, tum-bala, tum-balalayka
Tum-balalayka, strum balalayka.
Tum-balalayka, may we find joy.*

2 Maiden, maiden, tell me true,
What can grow, grow without dew?
What can burn for years and years?
What can cry and shed no tears?

3 Silly lad, here's the answer true:
A stone can grow, grow without dew.
Love can burn for years and years.
A heart can cry and shed no tears.

My Bonnie

Scottish folk song

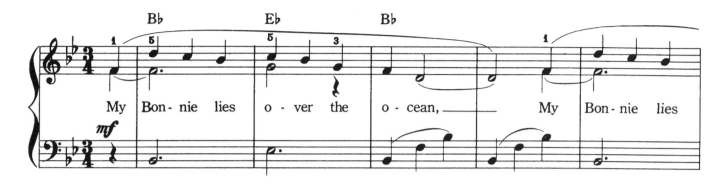

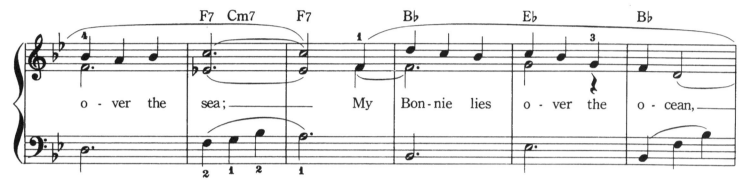

We Will Rock You

Czechoslovakian folk song

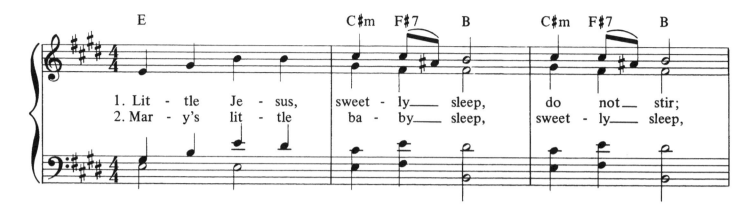

1. Lit - tle Je - sus, sweet - ly___ sleep, do not___ stir;
2. Mar - y's lit - tle ba - by___ sleep, sweet - ly___ sleep,

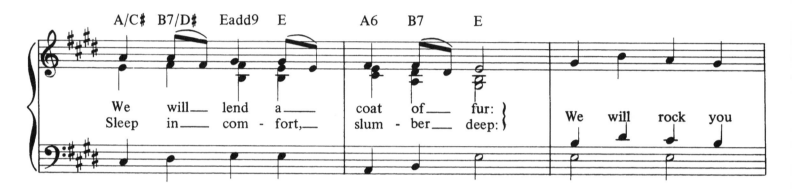

We will___ lend a___ coat of___ fur: We will rock you
Sleep in___ com - fort,___ slum - ber___ deep:

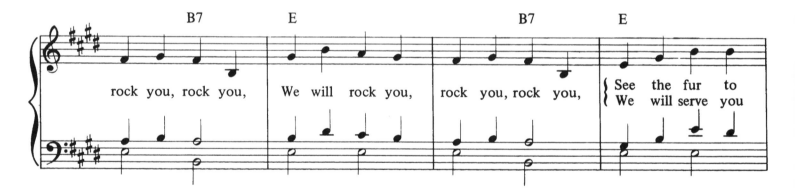

rock you, rock you, We will rock you, rock you, rock you, See the fur to
We will serve you

keep you___ warm, Snug - ly___ round your___ ti - ny___ form.
all we___ can, Dar - ling,___ dar - ling___ lit - tle___ man.

On the Bridge at Avignon

French folk song

Chorus:

2. The Abbes grave go This way;
   The ladies fine go This way.

3. The revelers go This way;
   The urchins bold go This way.

Hatikvoh
(The Hope)

Israeli anthem

Kol - od ba - le - vou p' ni - moh   ne fesh ye hu - di   ho - mi yoh,   ul

fa - a semis - roch ko - di - moh   a - in le - zi - von zo - fi - yoh

Refrain

Od   lo   ou - doh   tik voh se - nu   ha - tik - voh   ha no sho - noh

lo shuv le - e - rez a   vo - se   nu   lo ir bo   do vid cho   noh.

Holiday Songs

On the First Thanksgiving Day

On the first Thanks - giv - ing Day, Pil - grims went to church to pray,

Thanked the Lord for sun and rain, Thanked Him for the fields of grain.

Now Thanks - giv - ing comes a - gain, Praise the Lord as they did then,

Thank Him for the sun and rain, Thank Him for the fields of grain.

Over the River and through the Wood

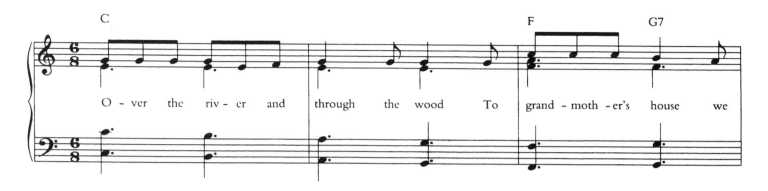

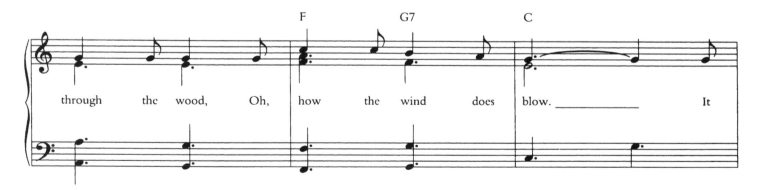

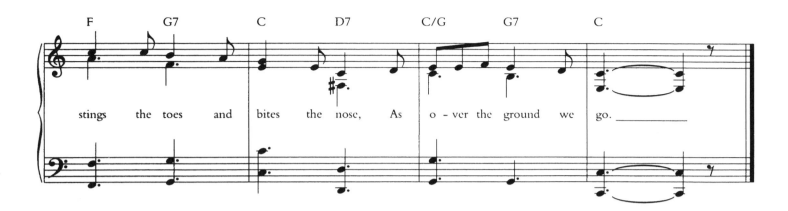

stings the toes and bites the nose, As o-ver the ground we go. _____

2. Over the river and through the wood,
To have a full day of play.
Oh, hear the bells ringing "ting-a-ling ling,"
For it's Thanksgiving Day.
Over the river and through the wood,
Trot fast, my dapple gray.
Spring o'er the ground just like a hound.
Hurrah for Thanksgiving Day!

3. Over the river and through the wood,
And straight through the barnyard gate.
It seems that we go so dreadfully slow,
It is so hard to wait.
Over the river and through the wood,
Now grandma's cap I spy.
Hurrah for fun, the pudding's done,
Hurrah for the pumpkin pie!

'Twas the Night before Christmas

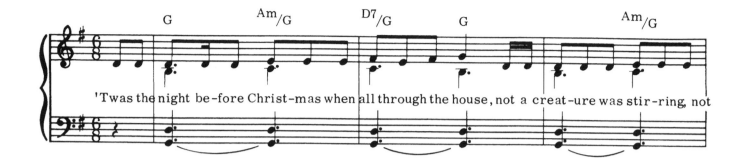

'Twas the night be-fore Christ-mas when all through the house, not a creat-ure was stir-ring, not

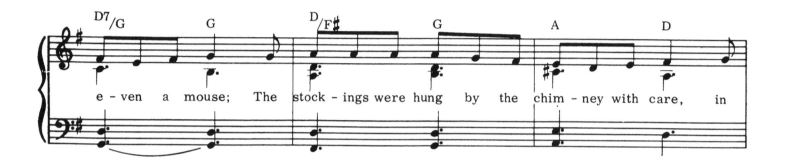

e-ven a mouse; The stock-ings were hung by the chim-ney with care, in

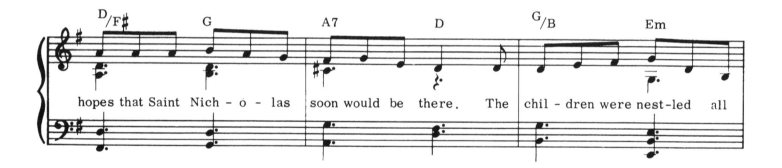

hopes that Saint Nich-o-las soon would be there. The chil-dren were nest-led all

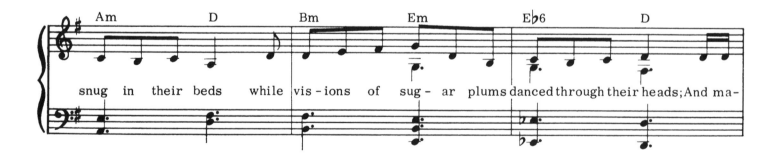

snug in their beds while vis-ions of sug-ar plums danced through their heads; And ma-

ma in her 'ker - chief, and I in my cap, had just set - tled our brains for a

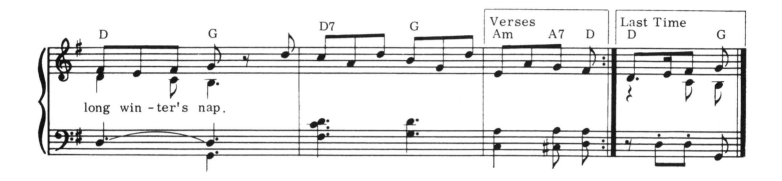

long win - ter's nap.

Verses

Last Time

Extra verses

When out on the lawn there arose such a clatter,
I sprang from my bed to see what was the matter.
Away to the window I flew like a flash,
Tore open the shutters and threw up the sash.
The moon on the breast of the new-fallen snow,
Gave a lustre of midday to objects below,
When, what to my wondering eyes should appear,
But a miniature sleigh, and eight tiny reindeer;

With a little old driver, so lively and quick,
I knew in a moment it must be St.Nick.
More rapid than eagles his coursers they came,
And he whistled, and shouted, and called them by name;
"Now, Dasher! now, Dancer! now, Prancer and Vixen!
On, Comet! on, Cupid! on Donner and Blitzen!
To the top of the porch, to the top of the wall!
Now, dash away, dash away, dash away all!"

As dry leaves that before the wild hurricane fly,
When they meet with an obstacle, mount to the sky
So up to the house-top the coursers they flew,
With the sleigh full of toys, and St.Nicholas, too.
And then in a twinkling, I heard on the roof
The prancing and pawing of each little hoof.
As I drew in my head, and was turning around,
Down the chimney St.Nicholas came with a bound.

He was dressed all in fur from his head to his foot,
And his clothes were all tarnished with ashes and soot,
A bundle of toys he had flung on his back,
And he looked like a peddler just opening his pack.
His eyes how they twinkled! his dimples how merry!
His cheeks were like roses, his nose like a cherry,
His droll little mouth was drawn up like a bow,
And the beard of his chin was as white as the snow.

The stump of a pipe he held tight in his teeth,
And the smoke, it encircled his head like a wreath.
He had a broad face and a round little belly
That shook when he laughed, like a bowl full of jelly.
He was chubby and plump, a right jolly old elf,
And I laughed when I saw him, in spite of myself.
A wink of his eye, and a twist of his head,
Soon gave me to know I had nothing to dread.

He spoke not a word, but went straight to his work,
And filled all the stockings; then turned with a jerk,
And laying his finger aside of his nose,
And giving a nod, up the chimney he rose.
He sprang to his sleigh, to his team gave a whistle,
And away they all flew like the down of a thistle;
But I heard him exclaim, ere he drove out of sight,
"Happy Christmas to all, and to all a Good-night!"

Hanukkah Song

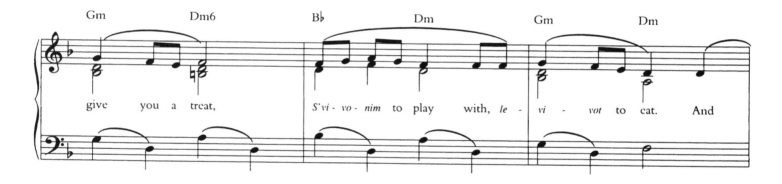

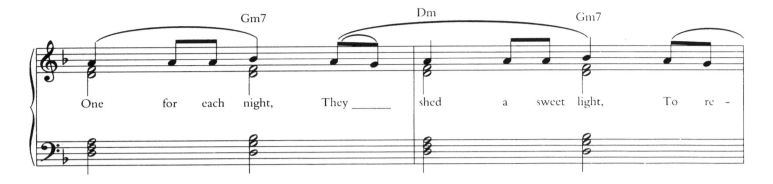

One   for each night,   They   shed   a   sweet light,   To   re -

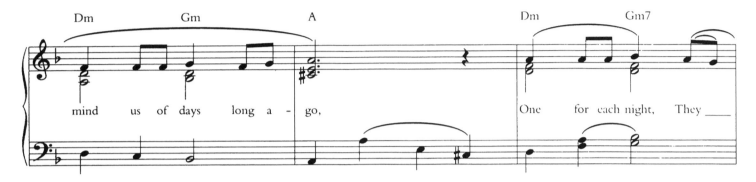

mind us of days long a - go,   One   for each night,   They

shed   a   sweet light,   To re - mind us of days   long a - go.

205

Christmas Is Coming

Christ — mas is com — ing! The goose is get — ting fat!

C   F   G7   C

Please to put a pen — ny in an old man's — hat,

C   F   G7   C

Please to put a pen — ny in an old man's hat.

C   F   G7   C

2. If you've no penny,
   A ha'penny will do,
   If you have no ha'penny,
   Then God bless you,
   If you have no ha'penny,
   Then God bless you.

The Friendly Beasts

2. "I", said the donkey, shaggy and brown,
   "I carried His mother uphill and down,
      I carried His mother to Bethlehem town",
   "I", said the donkey, shaggy and brown.

3. "I", said the cow, all white and red,
   "I gave Him my manger for a bed,
      I gave Him my hay to pillow His head"
   "I", said the cow, all white and red.

4. "I", said the sheep with the curly horn,
   "I gave Him my wool for a blanket warm,
      He wore my coat on Christmas morn".
   "I", said the sheep with the curly horn.

5. "I", said the dove from the rafters high,
   "I cooed Him to sleep so He would not cry,
      We cooed Him to sleep, my mate and I".
   "I", said the dove from the rafters high.

Repeat the first verse.

We Wish You a Merry Christmas

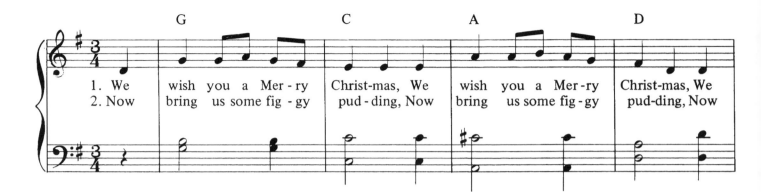

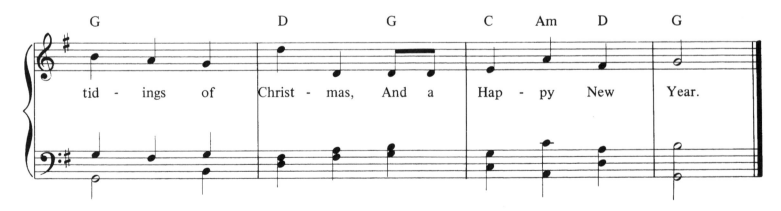

3. For we all like figgy pudding,
    We all like figgy pudding,
    We all like figgy pudding,
    So bring some out here.

    Chorus

4. And we won't go until we get some,
    We won't go until we get some,
    We won't go until we get some,
    So bring some out here!

    Chorus

Up on the Housetop

1. Up on the house-top the rein-deer pause, Out jumps good old San - ta Claus;
2. First comes the stock -ing the lit - tle Nell; Oh, dear San - ta, fill it well;

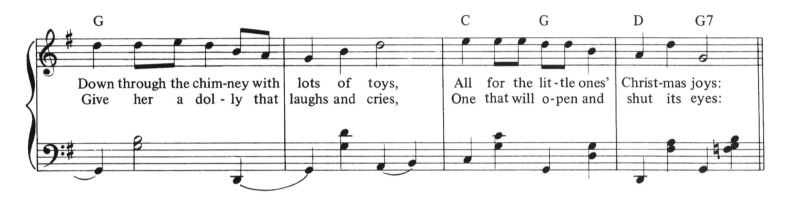

Down through the chim-ney with lots of toys, All for the lit -tle ones' Christ-mas joys:
Give her a dol - ly that laughs and cries, One that will o-pen and shut its eyes:

Chorus

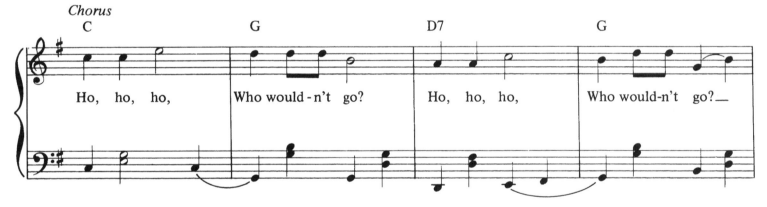

Ho, ho, ho, Who would -n't go? Ho, ho, ho, Who would-n't go?—

Up on the house-top, click, click, click; Down through the chim-ney with good Saint Nick.

3. Next comes the stocking of little Will;
    Oh, just see what a glorious fill;
    Here is a hammer and lots of tacks,
    Also a ball and a whip that cracks:
    Chorus

The Huron Indian Carol

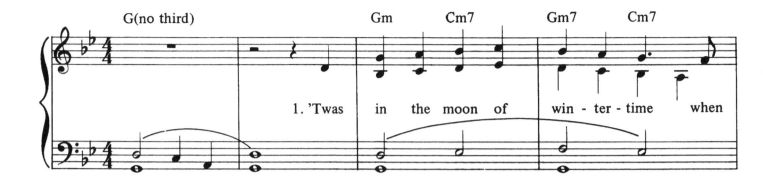

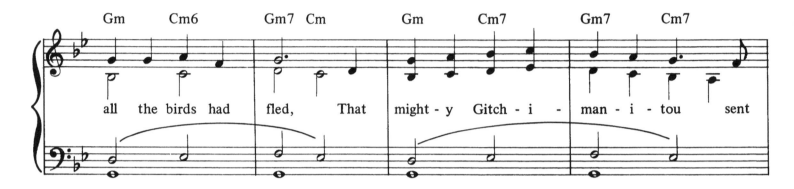

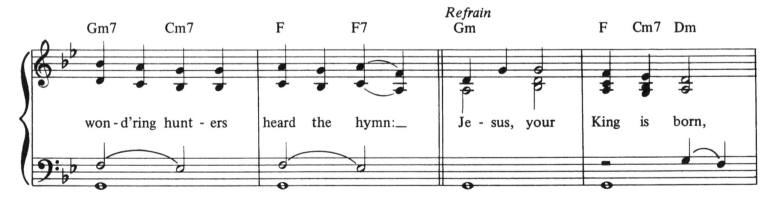

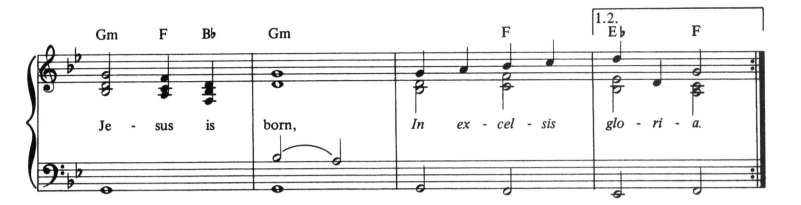

Je - sus is born, In ex - cel - sis glo - ri - a.

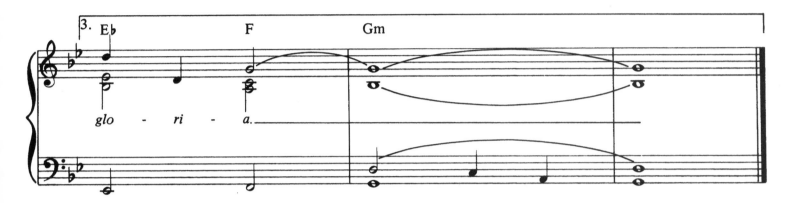

glo - ri - a.

2. Within a lodge of broken bark the tender Babe was
      found,
   A ragged robe of rabbit skin enwrapped his beauty
      round.
   The chiefs from far before Him knelt with gifts of
      fox and beaver pelt.
         Refrain:
         Jesus, your King is born,
         Jesus is born.
         In excelsis gloria.

3. O children of the forest free, O sons of Manitou,
   The Holy Child of earth and heav'n is born today for
      you,
   Come kneel before the radiant boy who brings you
      beauty, peace an joy.
         Refrain

Pat-a-Pan

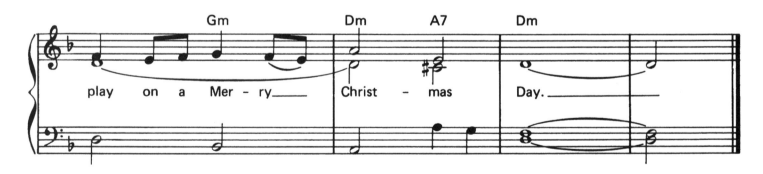

Now we'll play upon the drum and we'll make our voices hum,
    We'll be joyous as we play, Tu - re - lu - re - lu, Pat - a - pat - a - pan,
    We'll be joyous as we play on a Merry Christmas Day.

Just as men of other days raised their voices loud in praise, etc.

Brotherhood will rule and then peace on earth will come to men, etc.

Havah Nagilah

Ha - vah _____ na - gi - lah, ha - ah _____ na - gil - ah,

Ha - vah _____ na - gil - ah, vay - nis - m' - chayh.

Ha - vah _____ na - gil - ah, hav - ah _____ na - gil - ah,

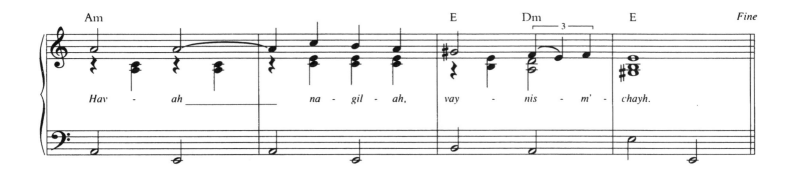

Hav - ah _____ na - gil - ah, vay - nis - m' - chayh.

Ha - vah n' - ra - ne - nah, ha - vah n' - ra - ne - nah,

Ha - vah n' - ra - ne - nah, vay - nis - m' - chayh.

Ha - vah n' - ra - ne - nah, ha - vah n' - ra - ne - nah,

Ha - vah n' - ra - ne - nah, vay - nis - m' - chayh.

U - ru, u - ru a - chim,
accel.

octaves optional to end

u-ru a-chim, b'-lev sa-me-ach, U-ru a-chim, b'-lev sa-me-ach,

U-ru a-chim, b'-lev sa-me-ach, U-ru a-chim, b'-lev sa-me-ach,

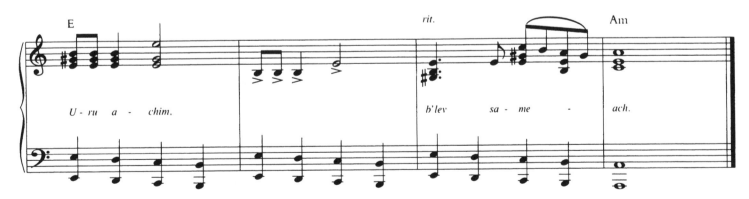

U-ru a-chim, b'lev sa-me - ach.

Away in a Manger

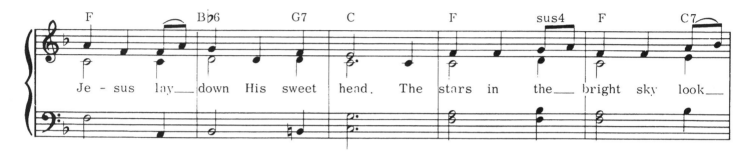

I Saw Three Ships

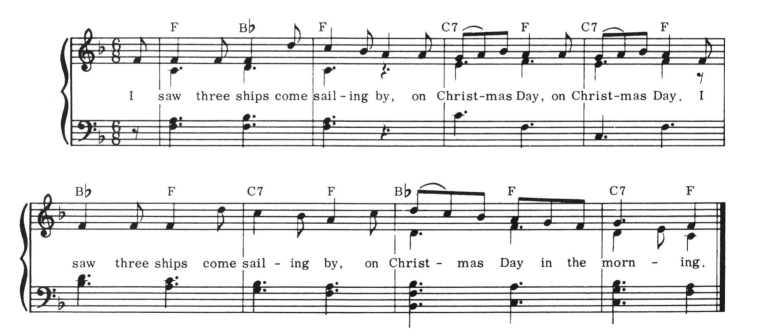

As Each Happy Christmas

As each hap—py Christ—mas Dawns on earth a—gain,

F   C⁷   F   C

Comes the ho—ly Christ—child To the hearts of men.

C⁷   F   Bb   F   C⁷   F

2. Enters with His blessing
   Into ev'ry home,
   Guides and guards our footsteps,
   As we go and come.

3. All unknown, beside me
   He will ever stand,
   And will safely lead me,
   With His own right hand.

I Heard the Bells on Christmas Day

mf

1. I heard the bells on Christ-mas day Their old fa - mil - iar ca - rols play, And
2. I thought how, as the day had come, The bel-fries of all Christ-en-dom Had

wild and sweet the words re - peat Of peace on earth, good will to men.
roll'd a - long th'un - bro - ken song Of peace on earth, good will to men.

Jolly Old Saint Nicholas

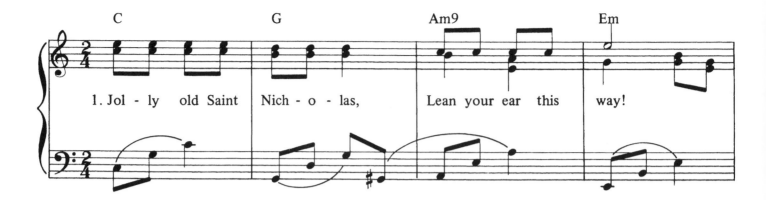

1. Jol - ly old Saint Nich - o - las, Lean your ear this way!

Don't you tell a sin - gle soul What I'm going to say;

Christ - mas Eve is com - ing soon; Now, you dear old man,

Whis - per what you'll bring to me; Tell me if you can.

2. When the clock is striking twelve,
When I'm fast asleep,
Down the chimney broad and black,
With your pack you'll creep;
All the stockings you will find
Hanging in a row;
Mine will be the shortest one,
You'll be sure to know.

3. Johnny wants a pair of skates;
Susy wants a dolly;
Nellie wants a storybook,
She thinks dolls are folly;
As for me, my little brain
Isn't very bright;
Choose for me, old Santa Claus,
What you think is right.

O Christmas Tree

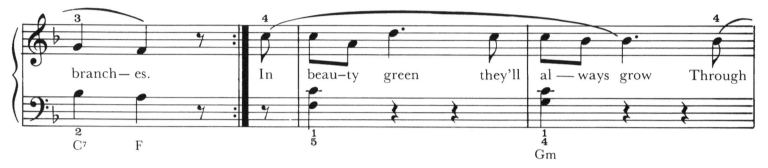

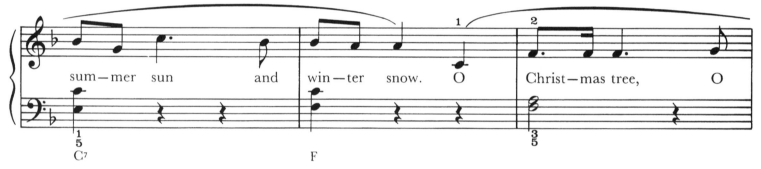

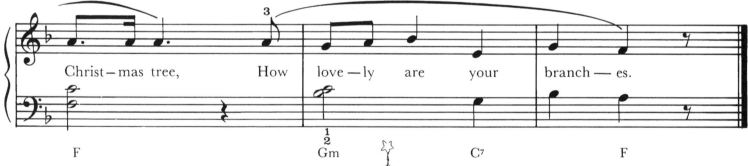

2. O Christmas tree, O Christmas tree,
Of all the trees most lovely;
Each year you bring to me delight
Shining bright on Christmas night.
O Christmas tree, O Christmas tree,
Of all the trees most lovely.

3. O Christmas tree, O Christmas tree,
Your beauty green will teach me
That hope and joy will ever be
The way to joy and peace for me.
O Christmas tree, O Christmas tree,
Your beauty green will teach me.

Red, White, and Blue Songs

Yankee Doodle

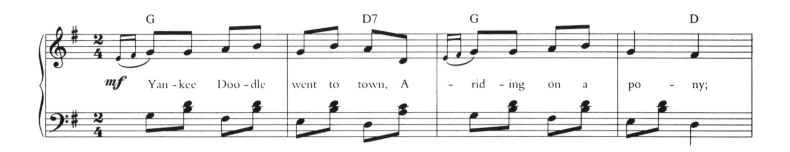

Chorus

2. Father and I went down to camp,
   Along with Captain Gooding;
   There we saw the men and boys,
   As thick as hasty pudding.
   Chorus

3. And there we saw a thousand men,
   As rich as Squire David;
   And what they wasted ev'ry day,
   I wish it could be savèd.
   Chorus

4. And there was Captain Washington,
   Upon a slapping stallion,
   A-giving orders to his men;
   I guess there was a million.
   Chorus

5. But I can't tell you half I saw,
   They kept up such a smother;
   So I took my hat off, made a bow,
   And scampered home to mother.
   Chorus

America, the Beautiful

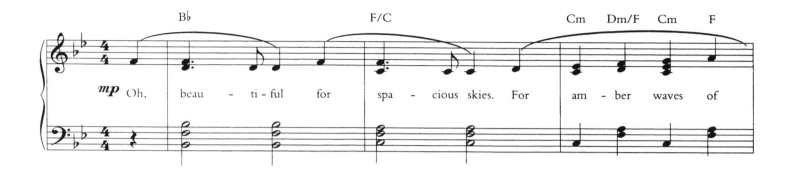

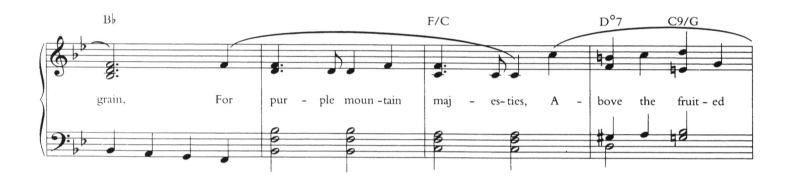

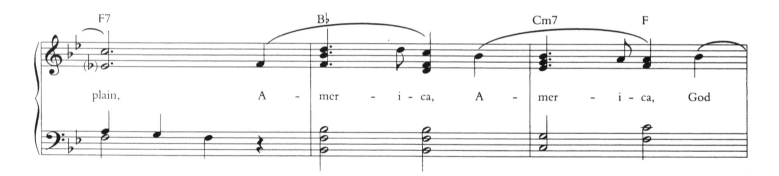

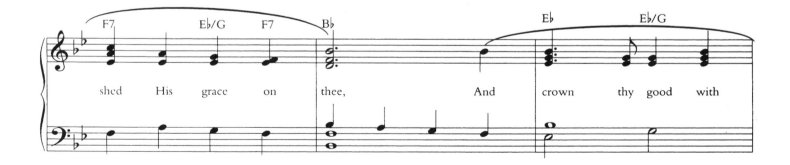

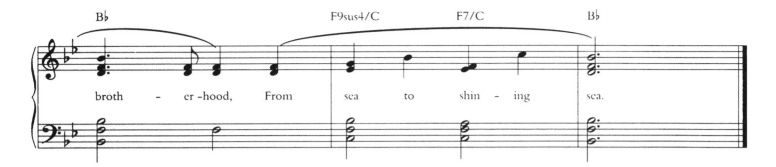

broth - er -hood, From sea to shin - ing sea.

2. Oh, beautiful for pilgrim feet,
   Whose stern impassioned stress,
   A thoroughfare for freedom beat,
   Across the wilderness.
   America, America,
   God mend thine ev'ry flaw,
   Confirm thy soul in self-control,
   Thy liberty in law.

3. Oh, beautiful for heroes proved,
   In liberating strife,
   Who more than self their country loved,
   And mercy more than life.
   America, America,
   May God thy gold refine,
   Till all success be nobleness,
   And ev'ry gain divine.

4. Oh, beautiful for patriot dream,
   That sees beyond the years,
   Thine alabaster cities gleam,
   Undimmed by human tears.
   America, America,
   God shed His grace on thee,
   And crown thy good with brotherhood,
   From sea to shining sea.

America
(My Country 'Tis of Thee)

2. My native country, thee,
   Land of the noble free,
   Thy name I love.
   I love thy rocks and rills,
   Thy woods and templed hills;
   My heart with rapture thrills
   Like that above.

3. Let music swell the breeze,
   And ring from all the trees,
   Sweet freedom's song.
   Let mortal tongues awake,
   Let all that breathe partake,
   Let rocks their silence break,
   The sound prolong.

4. Our fathers' God, to Thee,
   Author of liberty,
   To Thee we sing.
   Long may our land be bright
   With freedom's holy light,
   Protect us by Thy might,
   Great God, our King.

The Red, White and Blue

Rally Round the Flag

Oh, we'll ral - ly round the flag, boys, ral - ly once a - gain,

Shout - ing the bat - tle cry of free - dom; We will

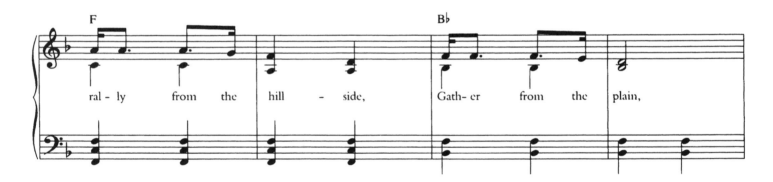

ral - ly from the hill - side, Gath- er from the plain,

Shout - ing the bat - tle cry of free - dom.

The Un - ion for - ev - er, Hur - rah! boys, hur - rah!

Down with the trai - tor, And up with the star; While we

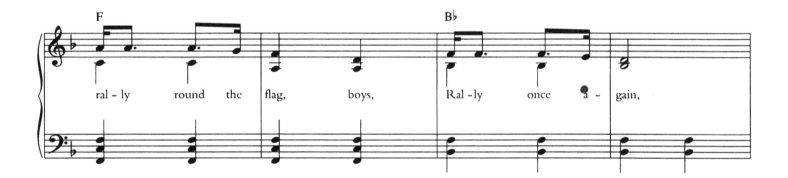

ral - ly round the flag, boys, Ral - ly once a - gain,

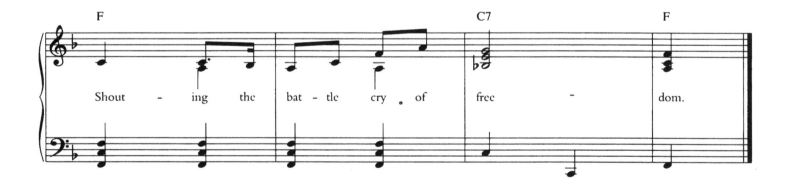

Shout - ing the bat - tle cry of free - dom.

2. We are springing to the call
   Of our brothers gone before,
   Shouting the battle cry of freedom,
   And we'll fill the vacant ranks
   With a million freemen more,
   Shouting the battle cry of freedom.
   Chorus

3. We will welcome to our numbers
   The loyal, true, and brave,
   Shouting the battle cry of freedom,
   And although they may be poor,
   Not a man shall be a slave,
   Shouting the battle cry of freedom
   Chorus

4. So, we're springing to the call
   From the East and from the West,
   Shouting the battle cry of freedom,
   And we'll hurl the rebel crew
   From the land we love the best,
   Shouting the battle cry of freedom.
   Chorus

Dixie

I__ wish I was__ in the land of cot-ton, Old times there are not for-got-ten, look a-

way, look a - way, look a - way, Dix -ie - land! In ___

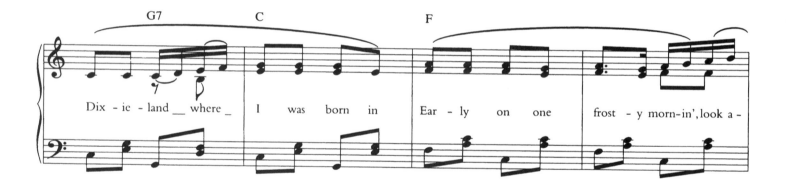

Dix - ie - land__ where _ I was born in Ear - ly on one frost - y morn-in', look a -

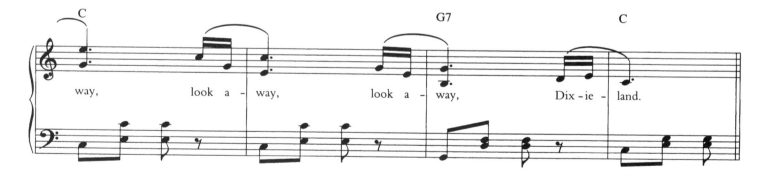

way, look a - way, look a - way, Dix - ie - land.

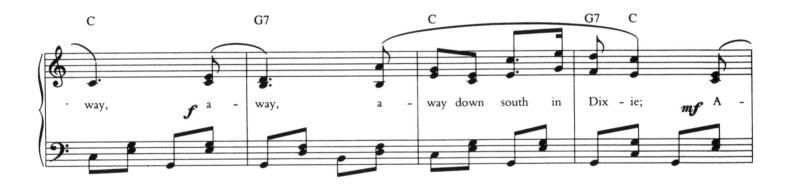

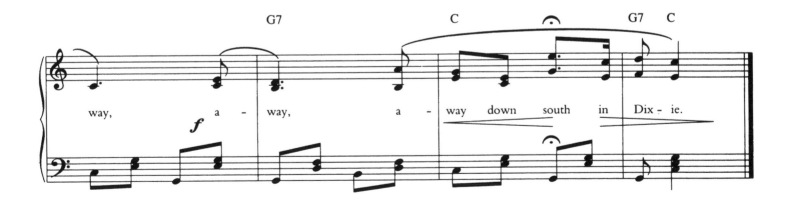

You're a Grand Old Flag

You're a grand old flag you're a high fly-ing flag, And for-

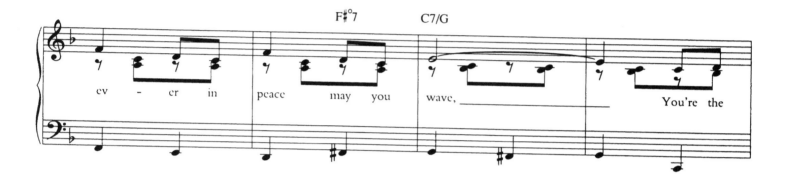

ev-er in peace may you wave, You're the

em-blem of the land I love, The

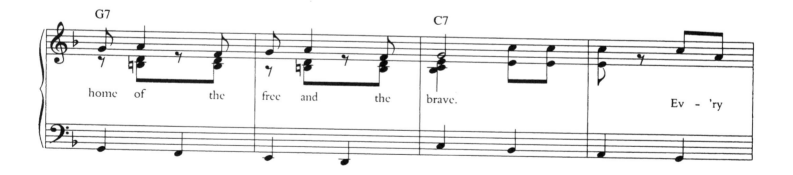

home of the free and the brave. Ev-'ry

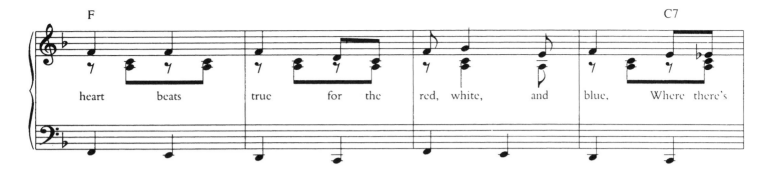

heart   beats   true   for the   red, white,   and   blue,   Where there's

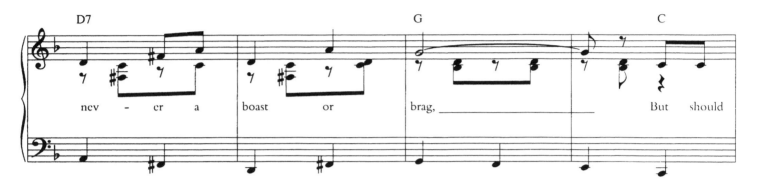

nev - er   a   boast   or   brag, _____   But should

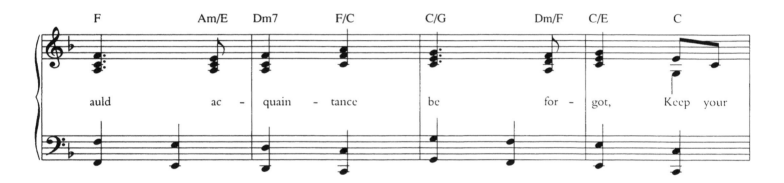

auld   ac - quain - tance   be   for - got,   Keep your

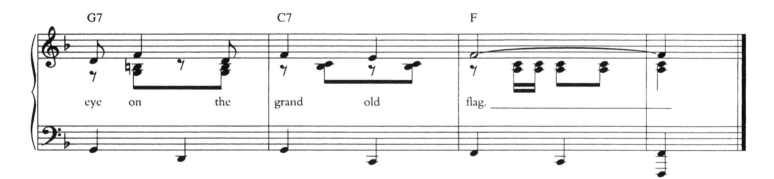

eye   on   the   grand   old   flag. _____

The Yankee Doodle Boy

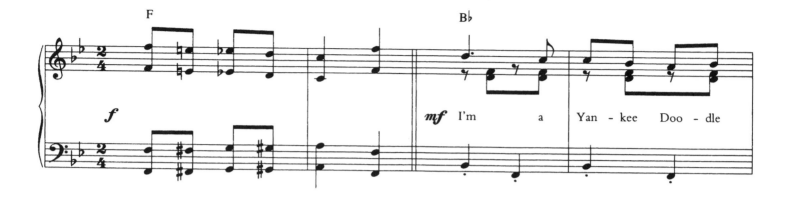

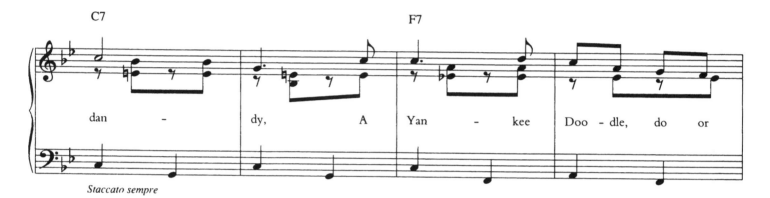

ly. _____ I've got a Yan - kee Doo - dle sweet -

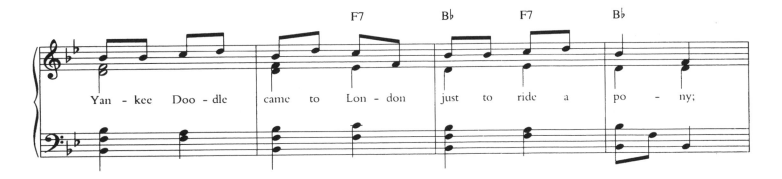

heart, She's my Yan - kee Doo - dle joy. _____

Yan - kee Doo - dle came to Lon - don just to ride a po - ny;

I am that Yan - kee Doo - dle boy.

The Star-Spangled Banner

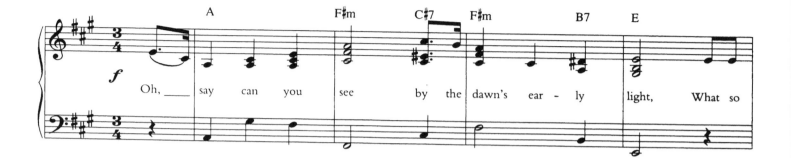

Oh, ___ say can you see by the dawn's ear - ly light, What so

proud - ly we hailed at the twi - light's last gleam - ing? Whose broad

stripes and bright stars, through the per - i - lous fight, O'er the

ram - parts we watched were so gal - lant - ly stream - ing? And the

rock - ets red glare, the bombs burst - ing in air, Gave

proof through the night that our flag was still there. Oh,

say does that ___ star - span - gled ban - er ___ yet ___ wave, ___ O'er the

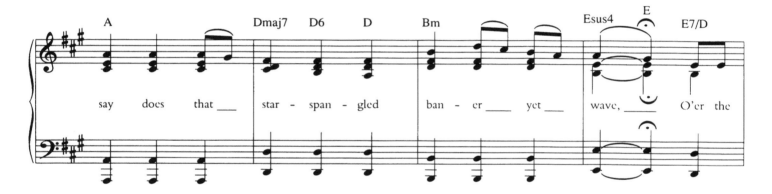

land ___ of the free and the home of the brave?

2. On the shore, dimly seen through the mists of the deep,
   Where the foe's haughty host in dread silence reposes,
   What is that which the breeze, o'er the towering steep,
   As it fitfully blows half conceals, half discloses?
   Now it catches the gleam of the morning's first beam,
   In full glory reflected now shines on the stream;
   'Tis the Star-Spangled Banner, oh long may it wave,
   O'er the land of the free and the home of the brave.

3. Oh, thus be it ever when freemen shall stand
   Between their loved homes and the war's desolation.
   Blest with vict'ry and peace, may the heav'n-rescued land
   Praise the Pow'r that hath made and preserved us a nation.
   Then conquer we must, when our cause it is just,
   And this be our motto, "In God is our trust."
   And the Star-Spangled Banner in triumph shall wave,
   O'er the land of the free and the home of the brave.

INDEX OF SONGS